Lessons that Last

Going into the school day with inspiration and reflection can help you feel more empowered and ready to take on the joys and challenges of teaching. In this refreshing book, Julie Schmidt Hasson and Laura Estes-Swilley provide 185 brief stories shared by former students about their most impactful teachers. With a different story for every day of the school year, the authors illuminate the many ways teachers shape students' lives. You can use them to set your intention for the day, to reflect on your teaching in the evening, or to infuse meetings and professional development with encouragement and affirmation.

Hasson and Estes-Swilley concisely unpack each story and pose questions to help you consider the meaning it holds for your own work. While the stories themselves are inspirational, they also provide models to help you make a greater (and more consistent) impact on your students' lives.

Through these daily reflections, you'll have the space to contemplate your practice and consider new perspectives and possibilities. With regular reflection, you can find greater satisfaction in teaching, particularly during challenging times. And as you grow, you'll have more capacity to help your students grow, too.

Julie Schmidt Hasson is a researcher, author, speaker, and big fan of educators everywhere. Julie's official title is Assistant Professor of School Administration in the Reich College of Education at Appalachian State University. She spent decades as a teacher and principal before becoming a professor. In addition to teaching graduate students, Julie conducts qualitative research in schools. Her research on teacher impact became the Chalk and Chances Project, which she founded in 2018. Julie's books, *Safe, Seen, and Stretched in the Classroom: The Remarkable Ways Teachers Shape Students' Lives* and *Pause, Ponder, and Persist in the Classroom: How Teachers Turn Challenges into Opportunities for Impact* illuminate the many ways teachers create ripples of impact.

Laura Estes-Swilley has been a high school English teacher for over 22 years, teaching several different literature and writing courses from Advanced Placement to remedial. Laura earned National Board certification in 2005 and was named Teacher of the Year at her school and English Teacher of the Year in her district. Laura's students have won multiple awards for their writing and poetry, and her fiction and poetry have been featured in several publications. Laura collaborated with the *Washington Post* for a report on teaching during the pandemic called "Dispatches from education's front lines" in the Fall of 2020. She is passionate about teaching and nurturing her students to become writers and readers who think for themselves.

Lessons that Last

185 Reflections on the Life-Shaping Power of a Teacher

Julie Schmidt Hasson and Laura Estes-Swilley

Routledge
Taylor & Francis Group

NEW YORK AND LONDON

Designed cover image: Studio Kitsch and Canva

First published 2024
by Routledge
605 Third Avenue, New York, NY 10158

and by Routledge
4 Park Square, Milton Park, Abingdon, Oxon, OX14 4RN

Routledge is an imprint of the Taylor & Francis Group, an informa business

ISBN: 978-1-032-43250-2 (hbk)
ISBN: 978-1-032-43126-0 (pbk)
ISBN: 978-1-003-36642-3 (ebk)

DOI: 10.4324/9781003366423

Typeset in Palatino
by Deanta Global Publishing Services, Chennai, India

To our students, who constantly challenge and inspire us.

Contents

Meet the Authors

Julie Schmidt Hasson

Julie Schmidt Hasson is a researcher, author, speaker, and big fan of educators everywhere. Julie's official title is Assistant Professor of School Administration in the Reich College of Education at Appalachian State University. She spent decades as a teacher and principal before becoming a professor. In addition to teaching graduate students, Julie conducts qualitative research in schools. Her research on teacher impact became the Chalk and Chances Project, which she founded in 2018. Julie's books, *Safe, Seen, and Stretched in the Classroom: The Remarkable Ways Teachers Shape Students' Lives* and *Pause, Ponder, and Persist in the Classroom: How Teachers Turn Challenges into Opportunities for Impact* illuminate the many ways teachers create ripples of impact.

Laura Estes-Swilley

Laura Estes-Swilley has been a high school English teacher for over 22 years, teaching several different literature and writing courses from Advanced Placement to remedial. Laura earned National Board certification in 2005 and was named Teacher of the Year at her school and English Teacher of the Year in her district. Laura's students have won multiple awards for their writing and poetry, and her fiction and poetry have been featured in several publications. Laura collaborated with the *Washington Post* for a report on teaching during the pandemic called "Dispatches from education's front lines" in the Fall of 2020. She is passionate about teaching and nurturing her students to become writers and readers who think for themselves.

Acknowledgments

Bringing a book to life is a collaborative process. We are grateful to Lauren Davis and the team at Routledge/Taylor & Francis Group for helping to transform our words into a beautiful book.

We've been blessed with unwavering support from our family and friends. To Brian and Jason, who support two passionate women. To Linda Angelilli, who modeled how to be a strong, independent woman. To Bill Estes, who made us laugh and encouraged us. To Bob Schmidt, who set us on the straight and narrow. And to Gayle Schmidt, who modeled extraordinary teaching.

Thank you to all the teachers who ignited our love of learning, to our colleagues who keep that fire burning, and to our students who inspire us every day, some of whom become our colleagues.

Most importantly, thank you to teachers everywhere for making the world a better place by shaping the lives of your students. In countless ways, every day, you make an impact.

Introduction

We've been friends for over 40 years, and for more than half that time we've been educators. When we're together, our conversations usually turn to teachers and teaching. Even when we were young students, we pondered what made someone a "good" teacher. What constitutes "good" teaching became a question we wrestled with when we were both new teachers, wondering if we were doing it right. And this question continues to captivate us as we support and mentor teachers. Questions around good teaching have long been a source of debate among professionals, professors, policymakers, and the public. Some advocate for using quantifiable factors, such as gains in achievement test scores. Others suggest using checklists of observable teacher behaviors. But these practices seem too narrow, and they don't capture the complexity and nuance of teaching. Most would agree that good teaching is characterized by impacting the learner. But this impact is not just relegated to academic outcomes, as teachers also impact students' social and emotional well-being. While it's difficult to define good teaching, it's not difficult to find evidence of it. After thousands of conversations, we've decided the truest evidence of good teaching comes from the students who have experienced it.

Over the past six years, Julie (a qualitative researcher) has interviewed hundreds of people about the teachers they remember. The stories people shared make the abstract notion of teacher impact more concrete. The stories also provide examples of the many ways teachers impact students' lives, and many center around small moments in a classroom. Teachers possibly wouldn't recall these moments or find them particularly noteworthy, but students carry the memories of these moments for years (or even decades) after they leave the classroom. A teacher's

DOI: 10.4324/9781003366423-1

demonstration of care, affirmation, or encouragement sends a powerful message to a student. We hope the stories we chose for this book send an equally powerful message to you, a reminder that you shape your students' lives in countless ways. They may not fully understand your impact until years later, and they may not be able to articulate how you've influenced them. But they know you have.

Teachers have countless opportunities to impact students' lives every day, but the rewards of this work come with significant challenges. Trying to meet the varying needs of a diverse group of young people takes incredible skill and commitment. Teachers at all levels of experience report feeling overwhelmed, and emotional fatigue can take a toll on a teacher's mental and physical health. Our hope is that the stories we provide in this book affirm the importance of your work and help you notice evidence of your impact. Knowing you're making a difference may give you the fuel you need to keep going.

While Julie contributed the stories, Laura (a veteran teacher) penned the reflections. Each story is unpacked, and the essence of the teacher's impact in the story is highlighted. Each reflection also includes questions to help you consider the meaning the story holds for your own work. While the stories themselves are inspirational, they also provide models for teachers who want to make a greater (and more consistent) impact on their students' lives. Reflection gives educators the space to contemplate their practice and consider new perspectives and possibilities. Regular reflection helps you grow so you can continue to help your students grow.

How to Use This Book

Pandemic challenges and systemic issues have led many teachers to experience a lack of hope and a loss of control. With long hours, a heavy workload, and seemingly impossible expectations, it's easy to fall prey to teacher burnout. Burnout can be described as a state of chronic stress that leads to physical and emotional exhaustion, loss of purpose, and feelings of inadequacy. It's difficult to experience the rewards of teaching from this disempowered place. A potential antidote to burnout is routine engagement with inspirational content and reflection.

We believe a morning routine brings a sense of calm and predictability, particularly during challenging times. Starting the day with an inspirational message can provide a strong foundation for peace and productivity. There are 185 entries in *Lessons that Last,* one for every school day (plus a few extra for planning days). Each entry contains a story and reflection about the life-shaping power of a teacher. Each entry ends with a reminder and celebration of your impact. If you choose to read a new story each morning, let it affirm how much your work matters, how much you matter. The way you feel in the morning can positively influence your emotional state for the rest of the day. A morning routine is powerful, but it's also personal. You may choose to go through each day's entry upon waking or with an early-morning coffee. You may choose to go through each daily entry in your classroom as you prepare for students to arrive or together in a morning meeting with colleagues. If mornings are hectic, you may choose to incorporate the stories and reflections into an evening (or perhaps a Sunday afternoon) routine. Experiment until you find a routine that works best for you.

While we designed this book with an entry for each school day, there are many other potential uses. Reading a story and using the reflection questions to facilitate discussion is a powerful way to start a meeting or professional development session. We have provided an index for this purpose with categories to help you find the right story for the right moment. The stories and accompanying reflection questions are also well suited for a faculty book study. We love the idea of an entire department or campus reading the same inspiring story on the same day. It creates an opportunity for discussion, reflection, and the sharing of our own school memories. Whether used individually or collaboratively, this book can be a catalyst for professional growth.

Regularly incorporating inspirational reading and reflection can help you become the kind of educator you want to be. As educators, the two of us have experienced the power of both reflection and a consistent routine, and we believe they can provide sustenance through these challenging times in our profession. We also believe in the power of connection, and we hope you will connect with other readers around the world through #lessonsthatlast on social media or by visiting the Chalk and Chances project at chalkandchances.com.

Our intention in creating this book is to elevate and celebrate teachers like you. We wish you a year of peace, joy, and satisfaction. And remember, in countless ways, every day, you make an impact.

Lesson 1
Creating Tradition

Family traditions are important as they are shared generation after generation. The same is true for your classroom traditions and celebrations, which students carry into the future. This story comes from Annie, who carries on a tradition from Mrs. Price's classroom:

> I have always loved birthdays. I love any kind of celebration. Perhaps that's why I have such fond, vivid memories of second grade. My teacher, Mrs. Price, had a knack for making each student feel special, especially on our birthdays.
>
> There was a chart in our classroom that displayed everyone's birthday. As each date grew closer on the calendar, we would all get excited. When someone's special day arrived, Mrs. Price would bring out a beautifully wrapped, flat package. The birthday student would open the package to find a new book for the classroom library. The student's name and the date were written on the inside cover, and he or she would get to read the book first. Those with summer birthdays were celebrated on their half-birthdays.
>
> On my birthday, I felt so important. I remember unwrapping my book and placing it in our library after reading it. What had always seemed like a day all about me became a day for all of us. Ever since second grade, I've been finding ways to bless others on my birthday. I'm grateful to Mrs. Price for teaching me how much fun that can be.

DOI: 10.4324/9781003366423-2

Reflection

Along with shared experiences, common traditions build community in your classroom. You signal the importance of occasions and moments by celebrating them, and your students wait with anticipation. The traditions important to you become important to your students, and they carry these traditions into adulthood.

What traditions do you remember celebrating in school when you were a student?

What occasions, achievements, or moments are important to celebrate with a class?

How do you encourage students to create meaningful traditions of their own?

You make an impact when you share celebrations and create traditions.

Lesson 2
Bringing the Light

You may not see the fears, doubts, and struggles that cast shadows on your students' lives, but never underestimate your power to bring the light. This story comes from Sarah, who remembers a stormy afternoon in Mrs. Hill's classroom:

> I grew up in Florida, where thunderstorms were typical on hot afternoons. The sky would grow dark, and the thunder would start to roll. The rain would begin softly then rapidly intensify. A particularly severe storm moved in one late September afternoon, an hour before dismissal, when I was in second grade. There was a loud clap of thunder as the power went out, and all the students shrieked. We all looked to Mrs. Hill to see if she seemed alarmed.
>
> Mrs. Hill never seemed alarmed, or even agitated. She was always calm and collected. So, it wasn't surprising when she motioned us all to come over and sit closely around her rocking chair. She pulled a flashlight out of a drawer and grabbed a book off her desk. With the flashlight propped up to light the pages, she began reading *The Magic Finger* by Roald Dahl. We were captivated and forgot all about the storm.
>
> I'm not sure why I remember that long ago moment so clearly. I just know that in the middle of that big storm, I felt safe. It was this little pocket of peace and joy in an otherwise chaotic situation. Now that I am a teacher, I think about Mrs. Hill often. I know my students are always watching me to see how I will respond to unexpected or stressful situations. I try to create a space of peace and joy inside our classroom, no matter what is happening outside.

DOI: 10.4324/9781003366423-3

Reflection

We all have the memory of a teacher who was happy to light the way for us. Many people don't see the fears that creep into children's lives, but educators know. It's easy to forget (especially on those days we feel like we're searching for our own light), but teachers are much more than curriculum and assessment. Take the time today to notice when and where you shine your light and how it makes the students around you glow.

How do you identify and understand your students' fears?

How can you bring a sense of peace and light to a stressful situation for your students?

How do you demonstrate peace and calm during stressful or chaotic times?

You make an impact when you shine light into the dark places.

Lesson 3
Being Brave

The beginning of a school year is an exciting (and often anxious) time for your students, but also for you. When you think about all that is ahead of you and your students, it can be hard to know where to start. This story comes from Chloe, who remembers the first day of school with Mrs. Gladden:

> I always had mixed emotions at the beginning of a new school year, simultaneously excited and nervous. I wondered if I would like my teacher, if my teacher would like me, and if I would enjoy learning with my new classmates. I remember my first day of fourth grade because my teacher, Mrs. Gladden, had a creative way of addressing my wonderings and fears.
>
> That day started like every other first day. We put our supplies away, introduced ourselves, and learned about the rules and procedures. But just before lunch, Mrs. Gladden pulled out a Question Box, and she gave us each a few index cards. We could write any question about our new teacher or new class and drop it in the box. We didn't have to put our name on our questions; so, I didn't worry so much about whether my questions would seem silly to others.
>
> At the end of the day, Mrs. Gladden patiently answered every question in the box. We learned that she never yells (except at her son's football games). We learned she tries not to give too much homework, and she rotates the classroom helpers. Looking back, I realize that I learned more about her from her choice to elicit questions and provide reassurance than I did from any answer she gave. I'm a teacher now, and I bring out my own Question Box every first day of a new school year.

DOI: 10.4324/9781003366423-4

Reflection

Your students are full of questions and concerns, but they start to get comfortable when they know who you are and what you expect. When you are planning your first week, you likely include lessons and activities designed to build community and knowledge of your students, but it is easy to forget to insert yourself as a participant and not just the observer.

How do your students get to know you at the beginning of the year?

How do you alleviate students' anxiety and fears?

What can you and your students gain by getting to know each other?

You make an impact when you make your students feel at ease by letting them know you.

Lesson 4
Extending a Welcome

The week before school starts is full of promise and excitement. Your students spend that time daydreaming of the kind of students they will be and wondering about the kind of teacher you will be. With the excitement and hopes, they have questions. This story comes from Alyssa, who remembers feeling welcomed to Miss Brindley's classroom:

> My family moved across the country the summer before I started fourth grade, and I was anxious about attending a new school. I worried more and more as the start of school approached. But then a letter arrived in the mail from my teacher, Miss Brindley.
>
> The letter had a picture of my new teacher with her dog. She shared several facts about herself (and the dog), and she seemed really nice. The letter also contained information about the classroom schedule, routines, and procedures. I read that letter over and over, and my anxiety began to turn into excitement.
>
> That sweet and simple gesture made a world of difference for me. Now I am a teacher, and I always send a welcome letter before the start of each school year. I include a picture of me (with my dog) along with information about the class. Thanks to Miss Brindley's example, when my students arrive, they seem a little less nervous.

Reflection

Finding ways to assuage the nerves of your students before school starts is time and effort well spent. You may build rapport before the year begins and help to build community before

DOI: 10.4324/9781003366423-5

students walk in the door. Just as you are wondering about them, they want to know about you, who you are and what and how they will be learning with you.

What is the value of extending a welcome to your new students?

What information do you seek about your students before you meet them?

How do you introduce yourself and your class to your students before school starts?

You make an impact when you anticipate students' questions as you welcome them to your class.

Lesson 5
Being Authentic

When you bring your true self to class each day, your students know – and they appreciate it (even if they don't always laugh at your jokes). This story comes from Cedrick, who remembers the happy environment in Mr. Colson's classroom:

Middle school was a challenging time for me. I remember trying hard to fit in but always feeling out of place. It felt like I had to constantly censor what I said and what I did for fear other kids would make fun of me. I had always been a silly, fun-loving kid, but I didn't feel free to be me in middle school.

When I arrived in Mr. Colson's math class on that first day, I noticed that he was wearing old Converse tennis shoes, and I stopped to read his T-shirt, which had the letter I, a heart, a picture of an apple, and the symbol for pi. He made funny comments to each of us as we came into the classroom. Mr. Colson even made going over the syllabus entertaining.

The thing I loved most about Mr. Colson was his propensity for dry jokes, what we would call "Dad jokes" today. For some reason, I remember all of them. Why do melons have big weddings? Because they cantaloupe. What happened when the cheese factory exploded? Da brie was everywhere. Mostly I enjoyed seeing the cool kids try not to laugh.

Mr. Colson was so comfortable being silly and being himself that we all felt like we could relax a little. His classroom was the one place I felt safe to be me. I remember it as a happy place, a welcome respite during a challenging time. I'll remember Mr. Colson as the one who showed me it's hip to be square.

DOI: 10.4324/9781003366423-6

Reflection

You set the tone in your classroom and build the community you desire through shared experiences. Whether your students are laughing or rolling their eyes at your jokes, your authenticity creates a connection. Within a community that honors authenticity, your shared space can be an oasis in your students' day.

What do you see as your most authentic traits and behaviors in the classroom?

What can students gain from your authenticity?

Why do your students look forward to coming to class each day?

You make an impact by simply being yourself.

Lesson 6
Being Memorable

We all have memorable teachers we seek to emulate, as educators, but also as people. What makes you memorable to your students isn't something you get to choose; it is part of who you are. This story comes from Cooper, who remembers his appreciation for Mr. Penz's axioms:

> Mr. Penz was my high school math teacher. He was tough but fair. The thing I remember most about him was his penchant for dispensing solid advice in simple statements. We referred to these as Penzisms.
>
> If we were trying to solve a problem with a solution that was way off, he would say, "That's as useless as a wooden frying pan." If we were slacking off and not doing work, he'd say, "The only thing that ever sat its way to success was a hen." My favorite Penzism was, "That'll stick with you like a hair in a biscuit."
>
> Sometimes I find myself repeating Penzisms to my kids. They look at me like I'm crazy, probably the same way we looked at Mr. Penz. But they'll remember those wise and witty sayings, and maybe they'll even reluctantly heed the advice, just like I did all those years ago.

Reflection

You are a teacher who will be remembered for your wisdom, quirks, character, humor, and kindness. Your students will remember your grace, strength, high expectations, and your steadfast support. There are as many reasons to recollect a beloved teacher as there are students. Take a moment to count

DOI: 10.4324/9781003366423-7

how many students you have taught and nurtured; you have made a difference in at least that many lives.

How many students have you taught in your career?

How do you think they remember you?

What would you like each student to remember about the time they spent in your classroom?

You make an impact when you share life-shaping advice.

Lesson 7
Creating Nostalgia

Remember a wonderful school year with a caring teacher. Many of us became teachers in an effort to recapture those feelings. Your students are building their own memory banks each day they spend with you. This story comes from Emma, who remembers her happy days in Mrs. Sabel's classroom:

I have so many clear memories of my first-grade class and my teacher, Mrs. Sabel. I think that's because of the pictures and artifacts my teacher saved and organized for me. At the beginning of the school year, Mrs. Sabel gave each student an accordion folder, which she called Keep Folders. When we completed a piece of writing or artwork we especially liked, we could add it to our Keep Folder.

Periodically, we went through our Keep Folders to cull our collections down to just those items we felt were most special. Mrs. Sabel was always taking pictures, and we often found new snapshots she had placed in our folders as well. During the last week of school, we were each given a scrapbook full of blank pages to be filled with items from our keep folders. I loved carefully gluing my pictures and artifacts in place and adding a brief description on each page.

Thirty years later, that scrapbook is still one of my most treasured possessions. The pages trigger happy memories of a year spent learning and growing under the care of a nurturing teacher. When I reunite with former classmates, we always bring our scrapbooks along to reminisce. My children enjoy looking through it, too, and talking about what school was like in "the old days." I'm so grateful that Mrs. Sabel took the time to create magical moments and lasting memories for me.

DOI: 10.4324/9781003366423-8

Reflection

You never know what might evoke a memory. Luckily, you have 180 days full of chances to create lasting impressions. When your students store memories of success and happiness, they walk away from your class with so much more than grades and bench-marks. With those memories, a wistfulness grows that turns into nostalgia for the days they spent with you.

How are you intentional with your students about holding onto their classroom experiences?

How do you want your class to be remembered by your students in 20 years?

Who in your classroom needs encouragement to make some memories?

You make an impact when you inspire students to hold onto memories from their days with you.

Lesson 8
Focusing on the Future

Students don't always see the long-term consequences of their decisions. This story comes from Marvin, who remembers how Mr. Schafer helped him stay on the path toward a brighter future:

By the time I got to tenth grade, I had lost all interest in school. I wasn't a terrible student, but academics didn't come easy for me. I knew I wasn't going to college, and I just wanted to start the next part of my life. My math teacher, Mr. Schafer, was one teacher who connected with me. He took the time to get to know me and was always encouraging. I was reluctant to tell him that I planned to drop out.

I finally got up the nerve to stay after class one day and tell Mr. Schafer my plans. At first, he just listened. Then he asked if he could give me some advice. He talked to me about the long-term financial benefits of graduating, even if I didn't go to college. He told me it would be much easier to stay and finish now rather than trying to get my diploma when I got older. He advised me to just stay through the end of the semester so that I would have a few more credits.

Although I had already made the decision to drop out, I agreed to finish the semester. I didn't want to disappoint Mr. Schafer. He checked in with me every day. He introduced me to the shop teacher and convinced me to stay for one more semester and take an electronics class. That class helped me realize I could have a future as an electrician. Each semester, Mr. Schafer persuaded me to stay longer, until I finally reached the end of my senior year. I have a picture of Mr. Schafer and me at my graduation on my wall. I'm grateful to him for never giving up on me.

DOI: 10.4324/9781003366423-9

Reflection

Marvin's story reveals two important lessons we all need to hear. One step at a time gets you where you want to be, even if you aren't quite sure where you're going. Also, a student's trust in a teacher is built on mutual respect. Every child needs a champion – one who doesn't judge but supports, one who is always on their side. You are a student's champion.

Which of your students might be losing hope in a brighter future?

Which of your students need a little extra support?

How can you encourage your students to commit to a future-focused goal?

You make an impact when you invest in your students' futures and inspire them to invest in themselves.

Lesson 9
Redirecting With Grace

All students need attention and validation, but some seek it in unusual ways. Your task is to determine how to minimize the distractions and maximize the learning. This story comes from Marc, who remembers Mrs. Rainey, the teacher who found a creative way to keep him on task and help him feel heard:

> I'm sure I drove my teachers crazy. I was always trying to make the other kids laugh. I loved jokes and funny stories, and I looked for any opportunity to tell them. My third-grade teacher, Mrs. Rainey, occasionally had to stop in the middle of a lesson and redirect the students around me because of my silliness.
>
> One day my teacher asked me to stay for a few minutes after school. I was sure she was going to give me detention or call my parents for disrupting the class. Instead, Mrs. Rainey had a plan. She said that if I got all of my work done and did not distract the students around me, she would let me tell jokes in front of the class at the end of the day. I ran home to work on my material.
>
> Every day I focused on completing all my work and made sure not to bother the other kids so that I could earn my reward. In exchange, Mrs. Rainey left the last few minutes of class for me to tell my jokes. I didn't fully appreciate her brilliance until I grew up and had kids of my own. It would have been easier to punish me, but her solution was much more creative and effective. I'm a pastor now, and although I take my preaching seriously, I always include a joke or two. I'm grateful to Mrs. Rainey for giving me grace.

DOI: 10.4324/9781003366423-10

Reflection

We all need grace now and again – and teachers give it away every day. When you give your students time and attention (despite their inappropriate ways of seeking it), you show that you value them. Even when they are being silly, they have something to say and, like all of us, a need to be heard.

How can you look beneath a frustrating behavior to find the deeper need a student is trying to fill?

How can you cultivate the patience and persistence required for giving grace to students who test you?

Who in your classroom needs some grace today?

You make an impact when you give students grace.

Lesson 10
Developing Character

Some of your students are naturally talented; they seem to be successful at everything they try. Others must work hard to succeed, and there is value in that struggle. This story comes from Gino, who remembers the rules for success in Mr. Gobel's classroom and team:

> Mr. Gobel was my tenth-grade history teacher and junior varsity baseball coach. He had high standards in the classroom and on the field. He had the same three rules posted in both places. Control yourself. Work Hard. Be coachable. I quickly realized that almost all my failures were because I failed to control myself, do the work, or listen.
>
> The truth is, I was never the most talented baseball player, but Mr. Gobel reminded me that a great attitude can make up for some lack of ability. He taught me the value of hustle and the importance of being open to feedback. I developed a strong work ethic and became a leader on the team.
>
> I didn't play baseball after high school, but I continued to use the lessons I learned from Mr. Gobel. Throughout my 20 years in the military, I focused on controlling myself, working hard, and being coachable. And I gave that same advice to the soldiers I led. I'm grateful to Mr. Gobel for building my character on and off the baseball field.

DOI: 10.4324/9781003366423-11

Reflection

In the talk of test scores, school grades, and measures of teacher effectiveness, something important can get lost. As a teacher, you are not teaching test-takers, you are teaching people who are growing and developing into who they will become. What students take from your class, in addition to curriculum, are building blocks of character and leadership.

What rules or expectations do you emphasize?

What do you do to help students become leaders?

How do you focus, either explicitly or implicitly, on character in your classroom?

You make an impact when your lessons help students develop strength of character.

Lesson 11
Challenging Norms

Students recognize their schools as microcosms of their communities and the world. Often, they look to you to help them make sense of what they see. This story comes from Shannon, who remembers how a discussion in Miss Gallant's classroom led to some life-shaping memories:

> I was a junior in high school when I took Miss Gallant's history class. We often talked about the racial unrest in our nation's history and the ways we could still see racial tensions in our country. Although I attended a diverse school, students from different backgrounds rarely interacted. Because of our discussions in Miss Gallant's class, we noticed the segregated way students often gathered in the lunchroom or out in the courtyard.
>
> When we brought this up in class, our teacher challenged us to find opportunities for students from different backgrounds to work together. With Miss Gallant's help, we decided to start a dance team. Because the dance team members had different cultural identities, each brought a different style of dance to the team. We learned from each other, and our choreography became a mix of our different styles.
>
> I have such happy memories of my time on the dance team. Working collaboratively with different kinds of people was a formative experience for me. I still connect with my former teammates, especially when I need a diverse set of perspectives. I am grateful to Miss Gallant for helping me appreciate the beauty of diversity, in dance and in life.

DOI: 10.4324/9781003366423-12

Reflection

Some things are hard to acknowledge in a classroom and community. But there are things we need to hear and address. By staying open and honest, you become your students' ally in important ways. A little guidance in the face of discomfort can have a lasting impact.

How do you create a culture open to real talk in your classroom?

How can you encourage students to look for solutions to the problems they see around them?

What are the conversations you should be having with students?

You make an impact when you courageously engage in important conversations with students.

Lesson 12
Teaching Civility

Many people think young people know things inherently. As an educator, you know better. Students must be taught the soft skills that will allow them to flourish in and out of school. This story comes from Nicco, who remembers the focus on civil discourse in Mr. Galt's classroom:

> I took a political science class in high school, and I enjoyed it. But recently, my appreciation for that knowledge (and the teacher who imparted it) has grown. Mr. Galt not only taught me about the branches of government, how policy works, and the process of elections; he also taught me how to have productive conversations around these topics.
>
> Mr. Galt frequently assigned an issue about which we would research and determine our positions. Then he put us into small groups to discuss the issue. Before the discussion, he always reviewed the civility rules, such as no interrupting and no personal attacks. A helpful list of response starters was on the board. For example, we could respond to another student's statement by saying, "I agree with you because …" Or, we could say, "I see it differently because …" Every argument had to be supported with facts and evidence.
>
> In our current political climate, I have longed to return to Mr. Galt's classroom. I miss the days when we could disagree about issues and still be friends. I miss my teacher's commitment to civility in political discourse. I know we could all benefit from Mr. Galt's rules and response starters. I'm certainly grateful to have learned those lessons from him.

DOI: 10.4324/9781003366423-13

Reflection

Nicco's memory provides us with a simple plan to create civility in the classroom. Your students want to be kind to each other, but sometimes don't know how, especially when they disagree. The more closely held an idea or belief, the harder it can be to discuss with someone who disagrees. Arming your students with the skills for civil discourse can be foundational to their lives.

How are you intentional about creating respectful dialogue in the classroom?

How do you encourage civility in your students?

When do your students wrestle with respectful communication the most?

You make an impact when you provide a foundation of respect and civility.

Lesson 13
Being There

There are times children and teens cannot be sheltered from the hardships of life, and they carry their personal lives with them into the schoolhouse. Often, you are the first to notice when a student needs a little extra attention. This story comes from Alex, who remembers Mr. Joseph, a teacher who became a steadfast influence in his life:

> I was in eighth grade when my father died in a car accident. It was a difficult year, and I felt really lost. My homeroom teacher, Mr. Joseph, made a special effort to help me. He often found me in the cafeteria before school and stopped to chat. He talked to me about my grades and made sure I kept attending my weekly meetings with the guidance counselor.
>
> Things got especially difficult when basketball season started. My dad had been my biggest fan, and he never missed one of my basketball games. I loved playing on the team, but I thought about quitting. When I stepped out onto the court for the first game of the season, I reluctantly looked up in the stands. My dad wasn't there, but Mr. Joseph was. He cheered for me and stopped to pat me on the back after the game.
>
> Mr. Joseph attended every game that season, and he attended many more games throughout the rest of my basketball career. When I graduated from high school, he wrote me a letter and told me that my father would be proud of me. Nothing could ever fill the void of my father's absence, but my teacher's presence meant so much to me. Mr. Joseph's support steadied me during that tumultuous time, and I will always be grateful.

DOI: 10.4324/9781003366423-14

Reflection

Many students deal with trauma and loss, and you know how much they need to feel supported and loved. Your students are grateful for you and the things you do that inspire them to keep going every day. You are a source of steadiness and encouragement in their lives.

Was there a time when you looked to a teacher for extra support and encouragement?

What do you do when you notice a student needs more from you?

Who in your classroom right now is dealing with trauma or loss?

You make an impact when you are there when your students need you.

Lesson 14
Mining Potential

You have many responsibilities during a single day, some more difficult than others. One of the most enriching parts of your job is seeing the potential in your students and encouraging them to grow. This story comes from Stacey, who remembers how a class job assigned by Mrs. Clarke helped her begin to see herself differently:

I was a painfully shy kid. I rarely spoke in class, and I definitely lacked confidence. So, when my fourth-grade teacher, Mrs. Clarke, announced the class helpers, I was shocked to learn I had been chosen as Milk Monitor. I doubted my ability to rise to the challenge. Milk Monitor required taking the milk orders in the morning, counting the money, taking the orders to the lunchroom, and distributing the milk each day at lunch. The position came with great responsibility.

When I got home, I told my parents about my new role. My dad worked at a bank, and he helped me devise a system for organizing the orders and counting the coins. I surprised myself with my efficiency and accuracy. I took great pride in being the Milk Monitor, and my confidence grew. When it was time to pick new helpers, Mrs. Clarke felt I should keep the job for the rest of the year.

Because Mrs. Clarke saw leadership potential in me, I began to see it in myself. Being the Milk Monitor was a small step in my journey toward building greater confidence. Through that challenge, I learned more about myself. I learned I was organized, reliable, and careful. I learned that others could depend on me. I am forever grateful to Mrs. Clarke for believing in me.

DOI: 10.4324/9781003366423-15

Reflection

Gaining confidence and understanding strengths puts students on a path toward future success. When you see the potential in your students, you are in a perfect position to help them see it themselves. Then you can encourage them to reach a little further and grow more with each risk.

How do your students respond to risks and new ideas?

How willing are your students to take social and academic risks?

What are some ways you inspire your students to reach their potential?

You make an impact when you see something special in students they didn't know was there.

Lesson 15
Coaching Teamwork

Functioning as part of a team does not come naturally to everyone. The classroom is one place where teammates are made, and that's a skill all students can use. This story comes from Finn, who remembers being humbled in Mrs. Lance's classroom:

> Mrs. Lance was my fourth-grade math teacher and the sponsor of our math bowl team. Math bowl is a competition based on solving problems correctly and quickly. Teamwork is essential, but in the heat of the competition, it's not always easy.
>
> There were a couple of domineering guys on the team. I was one. We tended to talk over the others, often overly confident in our answers. So, Mrs. Lance made a rule that we couldn't submit an answer until all four members of our team had a chance to speak. To our surprise, the quietest one on the team most often had the correct answer.
>
> That was a humbling experience for me, and a lesson that shaped the way I work with others. I learned that the loudest voices aren't necessarily right. Creating space for the quieter members of a team usually leads to a better solution. I'm grateful to Mrs. Lance for this lesson.

Reflection

Teaching your students to work as a team is part of building a culture that values all voices; it is also vital to their futures. While some students might believe it is easier to do things on their own, that attitude could work against them. As you ensure everyone has a place on the team in your classroom, you set students on a path to success.

DOI: 10.4324/9781003366423-16

How do you encourage team-building in your classroom?

How do you make space for quiet voices while still respecting the louder ones?

Why is practicing teamwork an important part of a student's education?

You make an impact when you teach students to value all voices and work together.

Lesson 16
Supporting Social Skills

A few words from a thoughtful teacher can change a student's day, year, or even life. This story comes from Jason, who remembers a treasured lesson on the playground from Mrs. Coates:

> I was always a very active and impulsive kid, which caused my classmates to pull away and avoid me. I remember feeling very sad and lonely one day during recess and sitting down on the bench next to my third-grade teacher, Mrs. Coates. When she asked what was wrong, I told her I didn't have any friends. She asked if she could give me some advice. Mrs. Coates explained that the best way to get a friend is to be a friend. She told me to carefully watch and notice when one of my classmates was struggling and to gently offer help.
>
> Later that day, I saw a classmate struggling to open the door with a stack of books. I quickly went over to hold the door for her. One of the boys forgot his snack, and I split my bag of pretzels with him. I realized that looking for ways to help others made me feel good, too. Before long, classmates wanted to work with me on projects and play with me at recess.
>
> Mrs. Coates' advice was life-changing for me. Paying attention to the needs of others and responding with kindness has been the foundation of my relationships for the past 30 years. I treasure my friendships, and I'm so grateful to my teacher for teaching me how to make friends and how to keep them. Mrs. Coates taught me life lessons that I continue to remember and use.

DOI: 10.4324/9781003366423-17

Reflection

It is painful to watch a student struggle socially and become isolated. With a bird's-eye view of your students, you can usually discern what a student needs. Through thoughtful seating, guided partnering for projects, or one-on-one coaching, you help students learn to form solid friendships.

Is there a place for everyone in the social groups you observe daily?

How can your students be more open to each other?

How could some coaching help the more isolated students in your classroom?

You make an impact by teaching students how to develop friendships.

Lesson 17
Working Alongside

You have much to offer your students, beyond your time and professional expertise. Your students are watching, listening, and learning from you beyond the bell. This story comes from Brent who remembers the life lessons he learned from Mr. Bronson outside the classroom:

> Mr. Bronson's agriculture class was my favorite in high school. I was interested in the content, but I also found Mr. Bronson interesting. He rarely taught through lecture; instead, we learned while working out in the barn and the field. He would give just enough feedback and advice to help us move along.
>
> One summer, Mr. Bronson offered a few of us the chance to earn a little money helping him repair some fencing on his own farm. While we worked, I asked him questions. I learned that his wife and young son died in a car accident years before. He didn't seem bitter. In fact, he talked about how grateful he was for the time he had with them. He told me how the accident taught him that most of the things that had bothered him were not real problems, just inconveniences.
>
> I learned important life lessons working alongside Mr. Bronson that summer. While we repaired the fence, he talked about doing the right thing, even when it's hard. He talked about investing in others and how that investment comes back to you in unexpected ways. He invested in me, and I'm sure he didn't expect me to return every summer to spend a few days helping him. But I did that until he finally sold the farm. I'm forever grateful for the wisdom he shared and for the impact he made on my life.

DOI: 10.4324/9781003366423-18

Reflection

Investing in young people is always wise. When you teach beyond the curriculum, you give your students wisdom that lasts a lifetime. Never underestimate the teaching that happens in the hallway, the bus ramp, or out in the field.

What do you think your students need to know beyond your formal curriculum?

What kinds of activities or conversations are your students missing in their lives?

How do you invest in your students?

You make an impact when you share your wisdom with your students.

Lesson 18
Friendly Encouragement

Teachers are cheerleaders. Your students need someone to remind them they can do it – whatever it is. And you get to experience the joy of their success. This story comes from Genelle, who remembers the encouraging environment in Mr. Sampson's classroom:

When I entered Mr. Sampson's math class on the first day of sixth grade, I noticed the signs on the walls. One said *Stay Calm and Problem Solve On*. Another one said *Divide and Conquer*. His sense of humor was disarming, and he immediately made me feel more at ease. He only had two rules: (1) You're never wrong; you just haven't gotten there yet. (2) Never ever take out a red pen in math class.

It was such a different approach. Mr. Sampson never marked anything wrong on our papers. He would just write, "Keep going." When I got stuck, he would ask me to tell him about my thinking. Talking through the problem was never scary, and I often found my own mistakes through his questioning. I began to feel less helpless and more confident.

Mr. Sampson's math class was a turning point for me. I began to think that I could do hard things. I began to realize that with the right attitude (and the right help), I could figure anything out. I have two daughters of my own now, and I try to model that approach for them. And thanks to the ripples of impact left by Mr. Sampson, they both love math.

DOI: 10.4324/9781003366423-19

Reflection

There is value in the struggle to learn, especially when a student is guided by a friendly hand. Confidence and self-sufficiency come from struggling through hard things in a safe and supportive environment.

How do you encourage students as they struggle a little in their learning?

How do you guide your students through their own mistakes?

Who needs to build some extra confidence in your classroom?

You make an impact when you guide students as they build confidence in their own abilities.

Lesson 19
Giving Empathy

You know there are some days when a student needs a break, and your compassion brings relief and restoration. This story comes from Shane, who remembers a tough day made a little easier in Mrs. Casey's classroom:

My grandfather died suddenly when I was in fourth grade. I didn't want to go to school the next day, but my mom had to help my grandmother. She must have called my teacher before I arrived because Mrs. Casey wasn't surprised when I came in and put my head down on my desk. She came over and quietly knelt beside me. She said that when I was ready to talk about it, she was ready to listen. She told me that I could participate as much or as little as I wanted in the class activities.

I tried to participate, but I just couldn't focus. I didn't even want to play with the other kids outside. During recess, Mrs. Casey brought me a stack of paper and some pens. She said that her father died last year, and it helped her to remember happy times with him. She told me that I could write about the happy times with my grandfather, if I felt like it.

I wrote all afternoon. I wrote about fishing trips and card games. I wrote about skipping rocks and catching worms. Remembering the happy times did help. At the end of the day, Mrs. Casey put all of my stories in a folder to take home. I shared them with my mom. She cried, but I think the stories made her feel better, too.

Since my year in Mrs. Casey's class, I've lost other loved ones. She not only gave me strategies for dealing with those losses, she became a model for how I respond

DOI: 10.4324/9781003366423-20

to those around me dealing with heartbreak. My teacher taught me so much more than academics, and I'm forever grateful.

Reflection

In hard times or sad times, your students look for your classroom to be a safe and supportive place. Even when they can't bring themselves to engage in the lessons and activities happening around them, your students are comforted by being with someone who cares for them and allows them to take care of their needs.

How do you know who needs some extra space to deal with what is happening in their personal lives?

How can you provide students with strategies to handle their feelings?

Why do you think students feel safe in your classroom?

You make an impact by helping students navigate grief and loss.

Lesson 20
Building Together

There are many benefits to building a classroom community; everything is easier when you are all working together. It is important for students to feel like they are part of something greater than themselves. This story comes from Jase, who remembers feeling supported in Mr. Shipp's classroom:

> Mr. Shipp was my high school history teacher, and I remember his class feeling like a community. He always said, "We sink or sail together." Many of my classes seemed competitive, but there was a spirit of caring and helpfulness in Mr. Shipp's classroom.
>
> When Mr. Shipp heard that I was running for class president, he made my campaign a collaborative activity. My classmates helped me create posters and flyers. They listened to my speech and gave feedback. When I won the election, it felt like a victory for all of us.
>
> I run my own company now, and I often think about the classroom culture Mr. Shipp created. I want my employees to feel that same sense of camaraderie and support. After all, in business and in life, we sink or sail together.

Reflection

Jase's memory is a reminder about the power of community. Creating community is intentional; you start with building the culture, then gradually release it to the students. You can be proud when they bloom into a group of supportive teammates who celebrate each other's successes and bolster each other in times of struggle.

DOI: 10.4324/9781003366423-21

How do you begin building classroom culture and community?

How do you feel about the culture in your classroom right now?

What is the purpose of building community in your classroom?

You make an impact when you guide students into creating a community of mutual support.

Lesson 21
Embracing Individuality

You already know every student is unique, with some special quality or talent that makes them distinct from the others – even if they don't realize it themselves. This story comes from Jennifer, who remembers Mrs. Tillman's classroom, where she finally felt special:

> As a kid, I was typical in every way. I was average in height and made average grades in school. My performance in extracurricular activities was unremarkable. But my third-grade teacher, Mrs. Tillman, always made me feel special.
>
> One day, during a science lesson on the human body, we used a black ink pad to stamp our fingerprints on a piece of paper. We examined them with a magnifying glass and compared them with our classmates' prints. Then Mrs. Tillman taught us something remarkable. She told us that no two people have the same fingerprints, not even identical twins. I still remember my teacher's words. "Your fingerprints are one of a kind, just like you. No one else has the same fingerprints. No one ever has, and no one ever will. There never has been nor will there ever be anyone else quite like you."
>
> I continue to be amazed by that lesson. I work in human resources for a school district now, and I help new teachers complete their background checks. Whenever I take an image of their fingerprints, I tell them about Mrs. Tillman and her lesson. I hope it reminds them of how special they are and of the opportunity they have to help their students feel special, too.

DOI: 10.4324/9781003366423-22

Reflection

You can help your students see what makes them special. When you open their eyes to their talents and unique qualities, your students can enact those gifts in meaningful ways as friends, spouses, parents, and professionals. Your influence has ripples in your students' lives.

What do you see that is special in each of your students?

What do you do to acknowledge and encourage your students' individuality?

Which students need to be shown they are special in your classroom today?

You make an impact when you see students the way they want to be seen.

Lesson 22
Leveraging Talents

As a professional, you know your students have talents and interests that can be encouraged and supported to maximize their learning. This story comes Charlie, who remembers an opportunity in Miss Dayton's classroom:

I was always doodling. Every blank space of my paper was filled with drawings and sketches. Miss Dayton seemed to realize that doodling helped me focus and learn, and she never scolded me for it. I remember a time when our class was studying the solar system. We had a packet to complete as we worked through each planet. I finished my packet early, and as usual, it was full of doodles. Miss Dayton checked it over to make sure it was complete and correct. Then she gave me some blank paper and suggested I create a comic book about the solar system.

I don't think I've ever worked harder on an assignment than I did on that comic book. I was drawing and writing every free minute. When I finished, I shared it with Miss Dayton. She enthusiastically praised my artwork and my writing. She even laminated the pages and bound them with a spiral binding. I'll never forget how proud I felt holding that comic book. Miss Dayton even let me share it with the other classes.

I still doodle on everything. And thanks to Miss Dayton, I love to create cartoons in my sketch books to delight my kids and my coworkers. My friends and family always receive my cartoons as birthday gifts. I am grateful to Miss Dayton for recognizing and encouraging this gift in me.

DOI: 10.4324/9781003366423-23

Reflection

When you aspire to engage your students by giving opportunities to use their talents, you find ways to engage them more fully. You customize assessment and improve the accuracy of the data you are collecting. And you have students who are happy to be learning in your class.

What student talents and interests do you see in your classroom?

What can your students accomplish when you leverage their talents and interests?

When do you enrich their learning by asking your students to share their talents?

You make an impact when you recognize and help students leverage their talents and interests.

Lesson 23
Engaging in Positivity

Most people respond to positive feedback, especially students. When you opt out of conflict and into relationship building, you set a firm foundation. This story comes from Chandra, who remembers Mr. Brennan's classroom where she finally had to let down her defenses:

> I know I was a challenge for my teachers due to my behavior and my academic struggles. By middle school, I had developed this tough posturing to protect myself from potential embarrassment. Often, my disrespect toward teachers or conflict with peers got me kicked out of class. And getting kicked out of class usually got me out of doing difficult academic tasks. But my tough kid routine didn't work with Mr. Brennan.
>
> When Mr. Brennan assigned a reading passage and a written response, he would walk around the room to check on students and offer support. I would say I wasn't working because I didn't have a pencil, and he would hand me a pencil and keep walking. He never argued or lectured, just smiled and moved on.
>
> One day, I ran out of my typical excuses. I told him I wasn't working because the assignment was stupid, and the book was stupid, and his class was stupid. He responded with, "Life is what you make of it." I'm sure he saw my eye roll. I was a master eye-roller, but he smiled and moved on to the next student. I was both frustrated and impressed that he didn't get into an argument with me.
>
> The day he handed back that assignment, he asked me to stay after class. Although I had only written one sentence, he complimented my work. He said I had the

DOI: 10.4324/9781003366423-24

start of an interesting response. He talked to me about the book and helped me outline the rest of my paper. I began to write more, and I began to look forward to Mr. Brennan's class. His class was a turning point in my life. It was a place where I wanted to engage rather than escape.

Reflection

There are times when engaging a student in class requires the long game. Your positivity, patience, and constancy go a long way toward building the respect and rapport your students desire. Even when it seems fruitless, every positive interaction or comment is a step toward building that bridge.

What messages are you sending through interactions in your classroom?

What do you do to avoid frustration and conflict with students?

Which students could benefit from patience and positivity right now?

You make an impact when you reach out to students with care and patience.

Lesson 24
Keeping the Faith

We all need someone who is always on our side. You are that person for many of your students, past and present. This story comes from Wyatt, who remembers Miss Dell's unwavering faith in him:

> By the time I got to high school, I had been playing piano for several years, but I was pretty green as a vocalist. My chorus teacher, Miss Dell, was choosing pieces for our spring recital. She asked me to perform a new song by John Hiatt called "Have a Little Faith in Me." She wanted me to sing it as a solo at the piano. I was completely intimidated by the song.
>
> After a few weeks of practice, I played and sang it for Miss Dell. It sounded awful, but she was not deterred. She just kept reassuring me that I would get it. Armed with her feedback, I continued to practice, but I had little belief that I would be ready for the recital.
>
> Miss Dell always challenged us to think about the emotion behind the songs we sang. She told us that to interpret a song well, we needed to feel it rather than just worry about the technical side of our performance. As I practiced, I tried to channel my deep appreciation for the people in my life who believed in me: my parents, my friends, and teachers like Miss Dell.
>
> When I performed the song in the spring recital, it was far from technically perfect, but it sounded pretty good. The audience responded to it, and Miss Dell cried. That song has come to mean more to me as I've grown older. It was lost on me at the time that Miss Dell was a living embodiment of that song. She had more than a little faith in me, and I will always be grateful for her.

DOI: 10.4324/9781003366423-25

Reflection

For some students, you may be the only person who believes in them, motivates them to succeed, and reassures them in times of struggle. Through the kindness and strength of your actions, your students can build the confidence you hope to inspire in them.

How do students respond when you are their champion?

How do you know when your students' confidence is growing?

What do you do to encourage and support your students?

You make an impact when you have faith in your students.

Lesson 25
Adding Some Fun

During the week, students spend most of their waking hours at school, making it like a second home. So, it's important that your classroom is a place of peace and happiness. This story comes from Bailey, who remembers the laughter in Mr. Winans' classroom:

> I always appreciated teachers who made school fun, the ones who gave me reasons to look forward to going. My fourth-grade teacher, Mr. Winans, certainly knew how to add a little fun to the school day. In addition to his dry jokes and crazy Hawaiian shirts, he loved to celebrate obscure holidays.
>
> We celebrated Talk Like a Pirate Day in September and Penguin Awareness Day in January. Mr. Winans would go all in and integrate the theme into every activity. My favorite was World Compliment Day in March. Just to make it more fun, he insisted we shout compliments in an angry voice. I clearly remember him aggressively shouting, "I really like those shoes!"
>
> School can become a bit monotonous and tedious at times, but Mr. Winans always found a way to make it interesting and fun. I loved his energy, his silliness, and his zest for life. My friends and I were in college when we learned that Mr. Winans had lost his battle with cancer. We got together to remember him. The memories made us laugh and cry. And of course, we celebrated our beloved teacher by shouting compliments.

DOI: 10.4324/9781003366423-26

Reflection

Your classroom is like a bell jar, where everything is shared and the energy you bring is magnified. When you project happiness, your students feel lighter. When you and your students are happy together, synergy and learning happen.

How do you create lightness and laughter with your students?

How do your students respond when the classroom atmosphere is light?

Who is your role model for creating the tone of your classroom?

You make an impact when you make your students' learning environment joyful.

Lesson 26
Captivating Learners

Students will tell you it is often the teacher, not the subject, that makes a class a favorite. When you have passion for what you are teaching, it spreads. This story comes from Celeste, who remembers Mr. McFadden, a teacher who taught her to reconsider things:

> I had never really liked history. I wasn't great at memorizing names and dates, and it seemed like history was a constant exercise in memorization. Mr. McFadden's history class was different. He taught history in stories. He asked us to think about protagonists and antagonists in historical events.
>
> Most importantly, Mr. McFadden taught us to consider why things happened. Why did countries end up in a war? Why did people participate in protests? Asking why helped me see the events that led up to a historical moment. It helped me consider the context around events. In Mr. McFadden's class, history was compelling.
>
> History became my passion, and eventually, my college major. Now I am a history teacher, and I try to make history come alive for my students. Mr. McFadden helped me see the humanity behind the names and dates. Learning to ask why helped me understand the past, but it also helps me make sense of the present.

Reflection

The best part of teaching is lighting a spark. When your students see the passion embedded in your daily lessons and feel the love you have for a subject or topic, they respond with enthusiasm. You bring the fuel to stoke the fire of your students' learning, creating their own intellectual passion.

DOI: 10.4324/9781003366423-27

How do you bring your passion for learning to your classroom?

How can you encourage a budding interest in your students?

What extra do you bring to the day when you are excited about what you are teaching?

You make an impact when you are a passionate teacher who inspires students.

Lesson 27
Setting Boundaries

One of the unspoken responsibilities of teaching is guiding your students in character development, which requires much from you as a person as well as a professional. This story comes from James, who remembers a lesson from Coach Waite in second chances:

> I was one of the biggest kids in my high school. The only thing bigger than my physique was my ego. I thought being a big football player allowed me to do whatever I wanted. I didn't always make good choices, and I couldn't see that I was really only hurting myself.
>
> One day at practice, I was harassing a teammate. When Coach Waite pulled me off the field to sit on the bench, I yelled inappropriately at him. I was shocked when he told me to clean out my locker and go home. The older players usually gave me a ride, and so, I had to walk the five miles to my house.
>
> I stopped at a convenience store on the way. I sat in front of that store filled with disappointment and regret until it got dark. A car pulled up, and I recognized the driver. Coach Waite told me to get in and said he would drive me home.
>
> On the way to my house, Coach Waite told me what he expected. He said that I had potential and was throwing it all away. I was still benched for the next game, but I could return to practice as long as I fulfilled the expectations. I was humbled by that experience, and it made me a better person. I am grateful to Coach Waite for believing I could change and for giving me the greatest gift, another chance.

DOI: 10.4324/9781003366423-28

Reflection

When you guide your students in social emotional learning and reinforce appropriate boundaries in classroom and peer interactions, you help your students grow into adults who can confront challenges and accept coaching. Your implicit lessons are as important as any formal curriculum.

What do you do to reinforce your own boundaries in the classroom?

What do you hope your students learn in your class about their own boundaries?

How do you coach students to help them see their own limits?

You make an impact when you are a role model for healthy relationships.

Lesson 28
Teaching That Echoes

You may never know how much your students have learned from you, nor what sticks with them. But your best lessons do resonate. This story comes from Autumn, who remembers how Mr. Tracey's lessons impacted her:

> I took an environmental science course in high school. Honestly, I took it because I thought it would be the easiest of the science courses offered. When I walked into Mr. Tracey's class on that first day, he invited me to stir up a big bucket full of dirt. I pulled up a scoop of earthworms. I never thought much about worms before, but Mr. Tracey spent that whole first class telling us why earthworms are critical to our survival.
>
> In the spring, he took us on a field trip to a pond to study the ecosystem. We looked at the tadpoles and the fish. We brought back water samples to study the microscopic organisms. I had no idea how much was going on in a pond. Mr. Tracey taught us about the ways humans endanger the delicate ecosystem of a pond, from litter to chemical runoff from fertilizers.
>
> I now look at the world around me with wonder and gratitude because of Mr. Tracey. I understand the interconnectedness of all living things, and I am aware of how easily we can mess up the environment. The learning from that one class continues to drive the choices I make every day. Because Mr. Tracey made an impact on me, I am more aware of the impact I make on the world.

DOI: 10.4324/9781003366423-29

Reflection

When they leave your classroom, your students will continue to carry your lessons. When you help your students become critical thinkers, when you introduce them to new concepts and perspectives, their minds expand in ways that continue to shape their lives.

How do you encourage thoughtful engagement in your classroom?

How do you envision your lessons rippling in your students' lives?

What communication from former students has inspired you?

You make an impact when your lessons resonate in your students' lives for years to come.

Lesson 29
Real-World Lessons

Students don't always see how they will use some skill or concept in the real world. When you connect their learning with real-world tasks, their learning is enhanced. This story comes from Carlos, who remembers an extra credit assignment from Mr. Graham that opened his eyes:

> I was struggling in geometry at the midpoint of the semester. Honestly, I just wasn't that interested in geometry, and I didn't see a need to learn it. I stayed after class one day to talk to Mr. Graham about my grade. He reminded me that an extra credit assignment was detailed in the syllabus. The assignment required students to interview someone who uses geometry at work and write a paper about it.
>
> When I got home, I asked my mom if she knew anyone who used geometry as part of a job. She gave me an exasperated look and reminded me that my dad worked for a construction company, and building a structure obviously required geometry. I was hoping for a more exciting prospect but decided to tag along with my dad the next afternoon.
>
> My dad was supervising a crew at a building that was almost complete. He showed me how they calculated how much floor tile to order and how they determined the layout of the tile. He talked to me about the angles of the trusses and how the crew built an arched doorway. When my dad was explaining the processes, all of the concepts that seemed so confusing now seemed clearer.
>
> When I turned my extra credit paper into Mr. Graham, I told him it was a pretty cool assignment. Students don't

DOI: 10.4324/9781003366423-30

always get to see how their learning can be applied in the real world. And, I had to admit that it made my dad seem pretty cool, too.

Reflection

It is a challenge to bridge the gap between the real world and the classroom. You can inspire learning (and even a new career goal) by revealing a real-world connection to the curriculum.

What skills or concepts didn't make sense to you until you put them into practice?

What could your students learn by connecting school to the real world?

How do you encourage students to connect what they learn in class to their lives?

You make an impact when you make learning relevant to your students' lives.

Lesson 30
Embracing Differences

We all long to be in spaces where we feel celebrated, not just tolerated. When you accept the kids who are different in some way, you show them you value them. This story comes from Brad, who is grateful to Mrs. Allen for letting him be himself:

> I was a quirky kid in high school. I had plenty of energy but lacked focus. I enjoyed doing unexpected stunts just to see people's reactions. I am certain that I drove my parents and teachers crazy. However, there was one adult who appreciated my eccentricity – Mrs. Allen. Her drama class was the perfect place to channel my creative impulses. Memorizing lines and waiting for my cues helped me focus. I also developed a deeper understanding of my emotions and found healthy ways to express them.
>
> Mrs. Allen started every class with improvisation exercises. We did these in pairs or small groups. Sometimes she gave us a situation, and we had to quickly jump in and start acting. Occasionally, she gave us a box of props and required us to pull something out and start using it. These activities taught me to think on my feet and to quickly appraise a situation. I had to carefully attend to the other actors and respond to their ideas.
>
> In all of my other classes, I had to tone it down, but Mrs. Allen allowed me to turn it up. I was encouraged to be bold and innovative. I became more confident and creative. I learned to work collaboratively with others and developed trust. I became the best version of myself.

DOI: 10.4324/9781003366423-31

Reflection

We all have a few students who stand out in our memories. Mrs. Allen's willingness to lean in and encourage her students' individuality is inspiring. When you are balancing the hundred responsibilities in a teacher's day, it can be easy to forget that students are also learning who they are and who they want to be.

How can you celebrate (not just tolerate) students' individuality?

How can you allow more expression of individuality in the classroom?

Who can you encourage in your classroom today?

You make an impact when you celebrate your students' individuality.

Lesson 31
Building Community

The culture in your classroom is always a work in progress, and it's likely something you think about every morning on the way to school. This story comes from Steven who remembers the spirit in Mrs. Alderman's classroom:

I was born with a missing arm. I got along just fine, mostly because my parents always treated me like any other kid. I lived in the same neighborhood from birth to age nine. Everyone knew me there. The summer before fourth grade, my family moved to a new town a few hours away. I was anxious about going to a new school. I wondered if people would stare at me or if kids would make fun of me.

I walked into Mrs. Alderman's class on that first day. She greeted me with a big smile, and most importantly, she treated me just like every other kid. She didn't make a fuss or try to help me with my supplies. She introduced me to Mike (the boy in the desk next to mine) and said she knew we would have much in common.

When class began, Mrs. Alderman called us all over to sit on the edge of the rug. She tossed a ball to each of us. We were to share something about ourselves and toss it back. When it was my turn, she tossed the ball just like she did to everyone else. I shared that I love playing baseball. One of the kids blurted out, "How do you catch with just one hand?" Instead of scolding him, she let me answer his question.

Mrs. Alderman was always reminding us that people have different ways of moving, learning, and being in the world. But we are still very much the same, and we all want to belong. She encouraged us to ask questions

DOI: 10.4324/9781003366423-32

instead of making assumptions about each other. I am forever grateful to Mrs. Alderman for helping me feel at home in a new place.

Reflection

Steven's heartwarming story is a reminder that you set the tone in your classroom. Your students look to you as a model and a guide for how to understand differences and exceptionalities. When you embrace differences, you help your students feel comfortable with others.

How do your students respond to change?

How do you bring new students into the community of a well-established class?

What do you hope your students learn from the differences in your classroom?

You make an impact when you show students how to embrace their peers.

Lesson 32
Finding More

There are times your students need something extra from you – tutoring, attention, care, or guidance. Some days you aren't sure you have anything in reserve to give, but somehow you find it. This story comes from Sondra, who remembers Mrs. Andrews, who inspired her by doing a little more:

> My father passed away from cancer when I was in first grade, and when I was in third grade, my mom got engaged to my stepfather. Mrs. Andrews showed compassion, asking me if I wanted to sign my papers with the new last name I was about to get when my stepfather adopted me. I was thrilled! While some adults didn't know what to say about my mom marrying again after such a terrible loss, Mrs. Andrews asked my opinion. She even came to the wedding.
>
> Another thing that I loved about Mrs. Andrews is the way we sang in class every day. We sang the multiplication tables each morning after singing "America the Beautiful." When I became a teacher myself, I carried on her tradition of singing every day in class. *And*, I made a point of going to at least one special event for each student every year. Whether it be a baseball game, a wedding, or a simple visit to their home. The impact Mrs. Andrews made lives on in my teaching.

Reflection

Your students may not realize how much you are giving or how you are supporting them, but they will. When you give a little extra, you are showing your students how much they matter. They will remember your kindness and support.

DOI: 10.4324/9781003366423-33

What do your students need most right now?

How do you support your students outside of the classroom?

Who in your classroom needs a little extra?

You make an impact when you help students feel important.

Lesson 33
Embracing Imperfections

There are no perfect educators, but there is power in your imperfection. This story comes from Alina, who remembers the beauty of Miss Wilson.

> I remember walking into Miss Wilson's class that first day and noticing the light patches on her skin. Later, I learned she had a condition called vitiligo. At first, I tried not to stare at her arms and face. But before long, her beautiful soul and contagious personality overshadowed her appearance.
>
> She captivated us when she read aloud, embodying each character. She had us on the edge of our seats during science demonstrations. She planned the best art projects and played the best music. I loved every minute of Miss Wilson's class.
>
> Mostly I remember Miss Wilson's big smile. She always seemed so happy. One day, love-bugs were swarming on the playground. They were attracted to the light spots on her skin and kept landing on her arms. She laughed so hard, and we did, too. Watching her laughing in the sun, I thought she was the most beautiful woman in the world.

Reflection

There is no doubt Alina learned many things that year in Miss Wilson's classroom, but the implicit lesson of self-acceptance might be the most important. Start with yourself today. Let Miss Wilson inspire you to be yourself in the classroom, remembering you don't have to be perfect to be wonderful.

DOI: 10.4324/9781003366423-34

What imperfections can you show students to model self-acceptance and self-love?

What do your students learn from seeing you as you are?

How does your own acceptance of imperfections empower and inspire your students?

You make an impact when you are the perfectly imperfect educator your students need.

Lesson 34
Making Flaws Fantastic

At times, we all want to blend into the crowd, but some find it harder than others. As teachers, we can help students see the value in being different. This story comes from Meghan, who remembers coming to terms with being different in Mr. Simms' classroom:

> As a kid, all I wanted was to be like everyone else. It seemed like nothing was built for me, not scissors or utensils or the string instruments in music class. I hated everything about being left-handed, until I met Mr. Simms.
>
> I remember my first morning in his class. He wrote his name on the chalkboard, and I noticed he used his left hand. I watched him carefully the rest of the morning. He took attendance, passed out papers, and used the stapler, all with his left hand.
>
> Throughout the year, Mr. Simms made a point to share facts about left-handed people, not just to me, but to the whole class. It turns out that we tend to be more creative, better problem-solvers, and even better drivers. Mr. Simms read a story about Buzz Aldrin, the left-handed astronaut. I noticed some of the boys trying to write with their left hands after that. I am grateful for the way Mr. Simms helped me see the gifts in being different. He made me feel proud of what I had always seen as a flaw.

Reflection

Helping students accept themselves can be a heavy lift, but it can also be as simple as a paradigm shift. You can help even the most self-conscious students see themselves differently. And, when you honor differences, your students will, too.

DOI: 10.4324/9781003366423-35

How did you build your own confidence to overcome insecurity?

How are your students handling their own concerns about fitting in?

Who in your classroom could use some extra encouragement today?

You make an impact when you help students accept (and even celebrate) who they are.

Lesson 35
Listening In

It's tempting to steer students away from controversy, away from tough questions, but asking hard questions is key to learning. In a community built on shared exploration, your students are free to ask and answer. This story comes from Tessa, who remembers learning to question in Mrs. Linn's classroom:

> I was always a proficient reader. I never remember struggling to decode the words. Reading was my escape, and I loved getting lost in the stories. But I became a different kind of reader when Mrs. Linn introduced me to *The Outsiders* by S. E. Hinton in seventh grade.
>
> When we began the book, Mrs. Linn instructed us to keep a journal of questions we had while reading. By the end of Chapter 1, my journal was already full of questions. I wrote questions about prejudice, about violence, and what makes people family. Before *The Outsiders*, I was often assigned questions about my reading that had literal answers, which could be found right in the text. The questions in my journal didn't have easy answers.
>
> Our class had rich discussions about the questions in our journals. Sometimes we disagreed, but Mrs. Linn never said anyone was wrong. She said that writers don't always give us the answers. Great writers often leave us with more questions. I credit Mrs. Linn for my continued love of reading and for all of the questions written in the margins of my books.

DOI: 10.4324/9781003366423-36

Reflection

When your students are engaged in inquiry, their hearts and minds are engaged. A question posed is an idea, a confusion, a concern brought to light. It can be scary to allow students to lead discussion by posing their own questions, but there is value in asking and listening to everyone's voice.

How do you encourage your students to question what they study?

How do you allow for student-led intellectual discourse?

Why is it important for your students to ask the questions about what concerns them?

You make an impact when you encourage students to question the world and their own perceptions.

Lesson 36
Extending Kindness

There are a hundred ways you can offer simple kindnesses to your students and their families. What matters most is your noticing and caring. This story comes from Jamie, who remembers a kind-hearted teacher, Mrs. Kemp:

> I was seven when my mom was deployed. My grandfather took care of me the year she was gone. He made sure I had all of the necessities, but he wasn't much of a nurturer. My grandfather never learned to read; so, he wasn't much help with my schoolwork either.
>
> One day, Mrs. Kemp was talking to our class about bedtime stories. I shared that I missed my mother reading to me. I told my teacher that I read to myself at bedtime, but it just wasn't the same. After school, Mrs. Kemp called my grandfather. She asked if I could listen over the phone in the evenings while she read to her own children.
>
> I loved listening to the stories my teacher read aloud. I held the phone tight, closed my eyes, and imagined the pages in the book. I laughed and asked questions along with her children. The loneliness I felt eased a bit. It was wonderful to feel like part of a family every evening. I never forgot Mrs. Kemp's kindness, and now, my favorite part of the day is reading bedtime stories to my own children.

Reflection

Compassion and kindness are the best gifts you can give. In a classroom filled with students, you can always find an opportunity to extend a little kindness. Whether a small gesture or

DOI: 10.4324/9781003366423-37

big commitment, the time and care you give your students are always appreciated.

What types of kindnesses do you like to receive during hard times?

What is the value of unexpected kindness and compassion?

How do you show care and compassion to others?

You make an impact when you share your kind and compassionate heart with your students.

Lesson 37
Inspiring Self-Assurance

Nothing helps a student overcome feelings of otherness better than knowing you have felt different as well. If you can do it, your students can, too. This story comes from Jacob, who remembers a teacher who didn't fit in, like him – Mrs. Wick:

> I grew up in rural West Virginia. The area was quite segregated, and everybody looked much like me. However, I felt different than my peers at school, like I did not fit in. Both of my parents were deaf, and neither could read nor write. They were unable to help me with academics, and I learned to read by watching closed captioning on television. My parents often depended on me to interpret for them in sign language. I was not a proficient reader, but I was a highly skilled sign-language interpreter.
>
> I will never forget my first day of seventh grade. I walked into my history class and was greeted by Ms. Wick, a petite black woman who stood out in the mostly white middle school. She started the class by posing the question, "What is history?"
>
> I thought about how I would interpret the word in sign language. I raised my hand, "His story – I suppose it is someone's story." The other students giggled.
>
> Ms. Wick smiled at me. "That is a very astute answer." Then she began to explain the origin of the word.
>
> From that moment on, I was hooked. Ms. Wick loved teaching about history, and I loved learning about it. We both felt like outsiders in that small town. We were different but, in many ways, the same.
>
> I carried those lessons from Ms. Wick through four tours in the Middle East. I now carry them into my own

DOI: 10.4324/9781003366423-38

classroom every day. I teach students with learning disabilities. I tell them it is ok to feel different – we all feel that way sometimes.

Reflection

Your students know when you are being honest with them, and they know they can trust you. When you are open about times you've felt out of place, you provide reassurance. They know who you are today and realize if *you* can grow confident, *they* can as well.

What made you feel like you didn't fit in with the people around you at times?

What helped you learn to leverage your differences as strengths?

Who do you see in our classroom having a hard time fitting in?

You make an impact by embracing your imperfection, giving students permission to embrace theirs, too.

Lesson 38
Sharing Wisdom

Your job consists of teaching, mentoring, advising, encouraging, and assessing – all designed to help students grow to their full potential and reach their goals. This story comes from Jane, who remembers Mr. Jenkins, a teacher who invested in her:

> I was a shy kid in high school. I took journalism because I liked to write, but I underestimated how much it involved talking to strangers. Mr. Jenkins had little sympathy or patience for my social anxiety. He always reminded me that I had to push past discomfort in pursuit of a story. After I completed an interview, he would ask, "Who do you need to talk to next?" He encouraged me to track down the right sources, not just the convenient sources.
>
> When a school policy about outside lunch seating was suddenly changed, I doggedly chased down administrators, student council leaders, and even the lunchroom manager. My persistence paid off, and I got to the truth. After I wrote the story, Mr. Jenkins carefully edited it. He reminded me that a skilled journalist doesn't just report a string of facts; she crafts the story in a way that engages the reader. He also helped me ensure that my facts were accurate and verified because trust is an essential part of quality reporting.
>
> Mr. Jenkins was just the right mix of toughness and encouragement. I still remember the wisdom he shared. He said that great stories are born of tenacity, not luck. He said that great journalists stay curious and hungry. He advised me to never operate from fear or favoritism, but to always work for the public interest. Those lessons have served me well.

DOI: 10.4324/9781003366423-39

Reflection

It takes a tenacious teacher to meet students where they are and guide them toward their goals. Your students benefit immensely from your willingness to expend energy in your classroom. Even if they don't fully value it in the moment, your students will hear your encouragement and wise words echo for many years to come.

What do you hope your students take away from being in your class?

What do you hope your students continue to hear from their time with you in 10, 15, or 20 years?

Why are you willing to devote your time, energy, and wisdom to your students?

You make an impact when you share encouragement and trusted wisdom with your students.

Lesson 39
Rewarding Growth

Many students need a reason to attempt a challenging task. They may need a little more motivation than progressing on to the next lesson or level. This story comes from Javi, who remembers the tangible rewards that helped him grow in Mr. Cronin's classroom:

> I was worried that I might be placed in Mr. Cronin's third-grade class. He was a stoic, bald, former military officer, and everything about him intimidated me. I was relieved to be placed with a very soft-spoken, sweet third-grade teacher. I felt unlucky when Mr. Cronin moved to fifth grade the same year I did, but ending up in his class turned out to be very lucky for me. Mr. Cronin had high expectations and challenged me to work harder and achieve more. I received services as a bilingual student, and I lacked confidence in reading. Mr. Cronin did not accept any excuses, and he believed in me.
>
> His military experience was evident in his classroom. He created three medals for progressing through three reading levels. I had never earned a medal before, and I wanted one so badly. I was determined to earn the first one, and I read for hours until I reached the first level. As I progressed, I gained confidence. By the end of the year, I earned the other two. I still have all three of those medals. They remind me that hard work pays off, even in academic pursuits.

DOI: 10.4324/9781003366423-40

Reflection

Your students may not yet have embraced the intrinsic rewards of learning. Some students are not motivated by a grade at the end of a quarter or semester because they need motivation right now. When you create clear rewards for meeting specific expectations, your students engage with learning in a meaningful way.

How do you set goals and rewards for yourself?

How can you bring some of what motivates you into your classroom?

What expectations in your classroom need rewards to motivate your students?

You make an impact when you reward, recognize, and motivate student learning.

Lesson 40
Making Musical Memories

You have creative talents that you pursue in your personal time, and they may have a place in your teaching practice. Your talents may delight and engage your students. This story comes from Nina, who remembers learning in Mr. Green's creative classroom:

> I remember my first day in Mr. Green's class. When other teachers were writing rules on the board, Mr. Green was pulling out his guitar. Instead of lecturing us about his expectations, he taught us a song about expected classroom behavior. It started like this, "I promise to always do my best in reading, math and all the rest." As the year progressed, whenever Mr. Green wanted us to remember something, he taught it with a song.
>
> I am amazed at the things I remember decades later just because Mr. Green put them to music. I can name the American Presidents and all 50 state capitals. Well, I can't say them; I have to sing them. I had difficulty mastering multiplication and division facts until I learned Mr. Green's collection of math facts songs. I still use that strategy today. Whenever I have to memorize something, I put it in a song.
>
> Some of my happiest memories from elementary school include Mr. Green and his guitar. He would sing silly songs just to get our attention and make us laugh. He would sing popular songs and invite us to sing along. "Puff the Magic Dragon" was a frequent sing-along request. Whenever I hear that song, it takes me right back to fourth grade.

DOI: 10.4324/9781003366423-41

Reflection

When you get creative, you are expanding your mind and nurturing your spirit. You may also be honing a resource for your classroom that can help you engage your students in meaningful learning. When you tap into your creative side, your students benefit.

What do you remember about the things you learned from an inventive teacher?

What are your creative talents?

How do you engage your students authentically?

You make an impact when you engage students in learning in a whole new way.

Lesson 41
Encouraging Growth

Your encouragement can inspire your students' aspirations. When you cheer them on, your students can accomplish anything. This story comes from Jennifer, who remembers feeling successful in Mrs. Rosen's classroom:

I loved picture books as a young child. I remember the book displays in my third-grade classroom, which Mrs. Rosen would change according to topic or season. She even had a special shelf where she would display several books by the same author along with the author's picture and personal facts. It was the first time I realized books are written by people, seemingly ordinary people, like my mom and dad. I was amazed to discover that the authors of the books I loved had pets and plants and lived in houses.

In the spring, our class learned about poetry, and poetry books filled Mrs. Rosen's displays. When it was time to write our own poems, I wrote about ants. Mrs. Rosen loved my poem and asked me to write it on a big piece of poster board. She let me draw an illustration on the bottom. I was thrilled when she took a picture and included it in our class newsletter. I was a real author, and my poem had been published!

I still love books and proudly call myself an author. Several of my short stories and poems have appeared in literary magazines. While it is always exciting to see my work in print, nothing will ever match the excitement of seeing that ant poem in the class newsletter.

DOI: 10.4324/9781003366423-42

Reflection

Your classroom is a place where students become inspired to try new things, where you have the power to support and bolster their learning and new talents. They need to know you believe in them. When you support your students' growth, you help them lay a foundation for their futures.

How did your teachers' support and encouragement impact you?

How do you inspire your students to try something new?

What are the ways you support and encourage growth in your students?

You make an impact when you encourage and support your students.

Lesson 42
Moving to Learn

Students learn by doing, especially when they have a thoughtful teacher with a bag of tricks. When your students engage in collaborative activities, they enjoy learning. This story comes from Trey, who remembers Mrs. Makenzie, a teacher who surprised him:

> I hated reading for most of my elementary school years. I was always active and social, and reading seemed like a painfully quiet and isolating activity. Taking turns reading out loud was no better. I would count the paragraphs to find mine and then daydream while the other kids were reading.
>
> All of that changed in Mrs. Makenzie's fifth-grade class. Every Friday, she arranged our chairs in a circle for Reader's Theater. We would read stories while acting out the scenes. Mrs. Makenzie chose students to play the characters, and she even added props. Laughter and applause filled the room. For the first time in my school career, I was completely engaged during reading time.
>
> Mrs. Makenzie also put us in groups to discuss the books we read. She always gave us questions to get started, but we would soon be deep in conversation. I realized that books are better when shared, and I discovered the best part of reading a great book is talking to someone else about it. Mrs. Makenzie started my lifelong love of reading. And, she inspired me to start a book club in every neighborhood where I've lived since.

DOI: 10.4324/9781003366423-43

Reflection

You have students who may be difficult to reach, but you have a bag of tricks to help engage all learners. Students respond when you show them different ways to learn, and there is nothing like physical movement to kickstart things. Hands-on learning brings to life what may otherwise seem dull.

What were your favorite learning activities when you were a student?

What can you bring to your students from your list of favorites?

When is it time to try something new in the classroom?

You make an impact when you engage students in a whole new way.

Lesson 43
Checking In

We all need a champion, someone who is always on our side, who wants the best for us. Someone who nurtures us and never judges. You are uniquely positioned to be this person for your students. This story comes from Ellen, who remembers Mr. Morrison, the teacher who cared enough to check in:

> I had always been a good student, especially in math. In tenth grade, I had Mr. Morrison for trigonometry in the morning, and I was his student assistant in the afternoon. As his assistant, I stapled study packets and graded quizzes while I listened to him teach geometry to the ninth graders. Mr. Morrison was so passionate about math that he engaged even the most reluctant learner.
>
> When I turned 16, my grades started to slip. I began spending time with a new group of friends, and school was not one of their priorities. I started skipping class and began to experiment with alcohol and drugs. I felt excited to be accepted by this group, but I also felt like I was losing myself.
>
> Mr. Morrison asked me to stay after class one day. He said that he was concerned about the changes in my grades and attendance. He asked me about my plans after graduation and my ultimate goals. Mostly he listened. I didn't feel judged, but Mr. Morrison's concern was evident. He talked about the potential he saw in me and the opportunities I might be giving up.
>
> It took me some time to get back on track, but by the beginning of eleventh grade, my academic performance was on the rise. I will always be grateful to Mr. Morrison for caring enough to have that difficult conversation with me. His words led me back to math and back to myself.

DOI: 10.4324/9781003366423-44

Reflection

It's important to be on a student's side. And it's not complicated: you need only to build relationships and extend unconditional acceptance. No matter how they are performing in your class, you are an important ally for your students.

How were you supported by someone who was always on your side, believing in you unconditionally?

How can you best support your students without judgment when they are struggling?

Who needs you to check in right now?

You make an impact when you care for and support your students unconditionally.

Lesson 44
Seeing Something Special

Each of your students has a different need – this is one of the challenges of teaching. But no matter their needs, they all deserve to be seen and valued. This story comes from Jordan, who remembers feeling valued in Mrs. Arbor's classroom:

I am the youngest of four children. Growing up, my sister was a gifted pianist, and both of my brothers excelled in sports. I was quiet and preferred reading to performing on a stage or field. At home, I always felt left out and left behind. Mrs. Arbor's class was the one place I felt special. Mrs. Arbor loved the same books I did, and we would sit and talk about the characters and themes. She often recommended new titles she thought I would enjoy.

On conference night, I sat between Mrs. Arbor and my parents, prepared for the usual explanation of test scores and grades. Instead, Mrs. Arbor pulled out a folder full of my written responses to the books I read. She told my parents that I was very insightful for my age. She pointed out my choice of words and phrases and complimented my ability to express my thoughts in writing. When the conference was over, I practically floated out of the room.

Mrs. Arbor took every opportunity to highlight my strengths in notes and phone calls to my parents. She didn't see my introverted nature as a disadvantage; she saw it as a gift. Her compliments facilitated the one thing I craved most, praise from my parents. Like most quiet kids, I was easily overlooked in a group, but Mrs. Arbor made the effort to see me.

DOI: 10.4324/9781003366423-45

Reflection

You get to appreciate students as they are while helping them grow. At times, you may see something in your students they (or their parents) have not yet noticed. When you share what you've noticed, you affirm their strengths and motivate them to do even more.

How did your teachers help you feel seen and valued?

How can you help students see in themselves what you have already noticed?

What special or interesting talents have you noticed in the students in your classroom right now?

You make an impact when you let students know you see something of value in them.

Lesson 45
Leveraging an Interest

Getting students engaged can be a heavy lift in a classroom full of students with a variety of interests. When you find a way to hook one of your learners, you can count that as a win. This story comes from Jeff, who remembers Mrs. Bryan, a teacher who capitalized on his interest:

> As a young boy, there were many things I liked about school, but reading was not one. I was capable, but not enthusiastic. Then I walked into Mrs. Bryan's classroom. The first thing I noticed was the enormous shelf full of books. We were encouraged to borrow a book to read when our assignments were completed. I decided to choose the biggest one on the shelf in hopes of impressing my friends. As I flipped through the pages of *The Encyclopedia of Insects*, I became fascinated by the detailed pictures of insects up close, and then I started to read the facts on the pages.
>
> Mrs. Bryan leveraged my love of insects by suggesting other related books in the school library. She even convinced me to check out a fiction book with insect characters. I kept *The Encyclopedia of Insects* inside my desk as a reference. On the last day of school, as we packed up our belongings, she handed me the book. She had written a note on the inside cover, "This belongs with you. Keep reading and keep learning."
>
> That book has had a special place on my shelf, and Mrs. Bryan has held a place in my heart for decades. She made me a lover of books.

DOI: 10.4324/9781003366423-46

Reflection

It's a relief when you finally discover what motivates a student. At times it's as simple as finding an interest and helping it grow. Their new interests and connections will stick with them long after they leave your classroom.

How do you find out about your students' interests?

How can you help them leverage their own interests in their learning?

What resources do you use to help students pursue their interests?

You make an impact when you help students make connections between what they love and what they are learning.

Lesson 46
Providing Resources

The students who walk in your door bring their own histories and perspectives, and it takes time and effort to learn who they are. It's worth the effort. This story comes from Elena, who remembers Mrs. Carter, a teacher who recognized the weight she was carrying:

> I had been at four different schools by the time I started second grade. I was behind academically and often felt frustrated and angry. I was no stranger to the office because I was frequently removed from class for yelling and throwing things on the floor. Lucky for me, the person who arrived to escort me out of class was Mrs. Carter, the guidance counselor. She had a fish tank in her office, and she let me sit and look at the fish until I calmed down. Then she began to tell me about each of the fish. "Look at how they breathe through their gills. I want you to try breathing like that, deep and slow." She taught me to take deep breaths, counting as the breath flowed in and out.
>
> From that morning on, I would sit by Mrs. Carter's fish tank every time I felt my emotions escalating. She was always there to listen. Honestly, she was the first adult I could count on. Mrs. Carter worked with my teacher to find ways to keep me in class. She would let me come feed the fish after school if I had a good day. She gave me some assessments to find out why I was struggling, and she found a tutor to help me catch up.
>
> I thought I was a bad kid, and so I acted like a bad kid. Mrs. Carter taught me strategies for coping with my emotions instead of acting out. She kept in touch with me even after I moved again. She sent me a letter when I graduated from high school and said she was proud of me. I could believe in myself because Mrs. Carter believed in me.

DOI: 10.4324/9781003366423-47

Reflection

You have many students in your classroom, all with their own unique needs. Some needs can feel overwhelming. Your students look to you (and your colleagues) for strategies and tools that bring peace and calm during difficult times.

What causes students to become overwhelmed?

What resources does your school community have to help students who are struggling?

How do you evaluate the needs of your students?

You make an impact when you notice what your students need and help them find it.

Lesson 47
Breaking Things Down

At times, students want something that seems out of reach. They need a mentor, an expert who is willing to invest some time. This story comes from Brent, who remembers the guiding hand of Coach Durbin:

> I always loved football. As I prepared for high school, all I wanted to do was make the football team. I made the junior varsity team as a freshman, almost everyone did – it was junior varsity. But my dream was to make the varsity team my sophomore year. I didn't.
>
> When tryouts were over and the roster for varsity was posted, I dragged myself, in despair and disbelief, into Coach Durbin's office. Coach Durbin was my physical education teacher and also one of the assistant football coaches. I shared my disappointment and asked him for advice. He told me I wasn't big enough. I wasn't fast enough. My understanding of the game wasn't deep enough. The good news was all of those things could be improved. Coach Durbin agreed to help me as long as I showed commitment and consistently followed the plan.
>
> He gave me a strength-training regimen and a new way of eating. He told me what drills to add to my daily sprints. He sat with me for hours watching videos of games and pausing to break down each play. A year later, my name was on the varsity roster. I continued to play through college.
>
> Coach Durbin taught me as much about life as he did about football. I learned from him the importance of setting a goal, breaking it down into action steps, and committing to it daily. Everything I have achieved has been built on that foundation.

DOI: 10.4324/9781003366423-48

Reflection

Your students depend on you to help them break big goals into small steps. Luckily, you are an expert at scaffolding skills and learning tasks for your students. As you teach, you are also modeling how your students can take ownership of their own goals and frame their own steps toward the big picture.

How do you break academic and personal goals into steps and monitor your progress?

How can you encourage students to put in the time to achieve the steps on the road toward their goals?

Why is it important that your students see models of goal setting?

You make an impact when you teach students to break big tasks and goals into achievable steps.

Lesson 48
Inspiring Outliers

As a teacher, you have often heard you should meet your students where they are. It's not always easy, but it's worth the effort. This story comes from Sean, who remembers being inspired in Mrs. Burnett's classroom:

> As a young child, I didn't feel like I belonged in school. I learned things quickly and easily, and I had a big appetite for books and information. So, when I started kindergarten, I was a proficient reader and knew how to add and subtract. I found no value in the letters and numbers lessons happening in my kindergarten class. If I had enjoyed art or outside play, I may have felt more excited about school. Those feelings persisted through first grade. I would quickly get through the work so I could take my book out and read.
>
> School changed for me in Mrs. Burnett's second-grade class. During math time, she would give me problems to solve. During reading time, she gave me baskets of books on different topics and let me write papers about what I learned. After I completed a paper about dinosaurs, she asked me if I would do a presentation for the class. She sent me to the computer lab to create slides and met with me to plan the talking points.
>
> I was nervous and excited as I stood in front of the class and explained the difference between carnivores and herbivores. The other kids started raising their hands and asking questions. I experienced an amazing sense of synergy and suddenly felt like a valuable member of the class. My presentations became a regular part of science time, and I became hooked on teaching. Mrs. Burnett helped me see that the best part about learning something new is sharing that learning with others.

DOI: 10.4324/9781003366423-49

Reflection

Engaging a student who is an outlier requires creative thinking and an ample bag of tricks. In the end, how you engage your students is not as important as helping them feel part of a community of learners.

Who are the outliers in your classroom in need of some encouragement?

Who inspired you as a student by meeting you where you were?

What are your go-to strategies for engaging disconnected students?

You make an impact when you inspire students to become involved learners.

Lesson 49
Making Memories

You work diligently planning, preparing, teaching, and assessing while your students are hard at work thinking, learning, growing, and developing. It can be difficult to step back and have fun. This story comes from Paul, who remembers a quick change of plans in Mrs. Whitley's classroom:

I grew up in Texas, where it rarely snows. But one cold December morning when I was ten, I woke up to a couple of inches of snow on the ground. I was so disappointed when my mom said I still had to go to school. I wanted so badly just to play outside. When I walked into Mrs. Whitley's fifth-grade classroom, she was erasing the morning work on the board. She replaced the usual math problems with one sentence: "Put your coat back on and meet me outside."

One by one, my classmates made their way out to the playground where they found Mrs. Whitley and me trying to make snowballs. We played outside most of the morning, chasing each other and making snow angels. I think our teacher had as much fun as we did. When we went back inside, Mrs. Whitley made us hot chocolate.

I cherish the memory of that morning, and I'm so grateful Mrs. Whitley chose to pause the learning and play. Honestly, some important learning still happened that day. I learned that sometimes work can wait. Snow melts and children grow, and if you aren't careful, you'll miss the chance to make a memory.

DOI: 10.4324/9781003366423-50

Reflection

While you do spend all day with students, your primary focus is on the joy of acquiring knowledge and mastering skills. But there is also value in making some memories your scholars can hold in their hearts. After all, the students before you will only be this age and at this developmental stage once, with you as a guide.

What do you want to remember about the times you spend with your students this year?

What do you want your students to remember about the year they spend with you?

How do you create joyful memories with your students?

You make an impact when you share fun moments with your students as you teach them.

Lesson 50
Fostering Leadership

Some students are viewed as leaders by their peers, and teachers know how to leverage student leadership to help others in the classroom. This story comes from Ben, who shared a leadership lesson he learned in Mrs. Greenlee's classroom:

Life was pretty easy for me as a ten-year-old. As the youngest of four boys, I got some credibility from my older brothers, all known as exceptional athletes. My oldest brother was the high school quarterback that year. I was tall for my age, and my sport of choice was basketball. Every day at recess, my buddies and I went straight to the court. I dominated those playground pick-up games.

Most of the kids in my class had been together since kindergarten. We had always been friends, but things started to shift a little in fifth grade. We began to sort ourselves into groups, and a hierarchy formed based on popularity. Marcus was always a bit different. He was small and wore thick glasses. He was awkward both physically and socially. The boys started calling him "Mucus," and they made sure he never touched the basketball during recess. I did not actively torment Marcus, but I did sometimes laugh.

One afternoon as we were packing up to go home, Mrs. Greenlee asked me to stay behind. She told me she was concerned about Marcus because he seemed isolated and sad. She suspected that the other boys were teasing him. I was prepared to be scolded for laughing, but instead, she said something that surprised me. Mrs. Greenlee said, "I've noticed that the other students look up to you. They watch what you do, and they follow your lead. I wonder if you could find a way to include Marcus and help him feel

DOI: 10.4324/9781003366423-51

more accepted." I thought about her words all the way home.

The next day at recess, I picked Marcus to be on my team. When another boy chanted "Mucus," I asked him to stop. I talked to Marcus as we walked back into the classroom. As I got to my seat, Mrs. Greenlee smiled at me. It felt good to do the right thing, and it felt even better to know that I made Mrs. Greenlee proud.

Reflection

Mrs. Greenlee taught Ben that with privilege comes responsibility. Marcus, the other boys, and even the younger kids all benefited from one prudent conversation. Students often lament that they aren't learning things they can use in life, but they just haven't realized the important lessons that were quietly taught in and out of the classroom.

How do you identify the leaders in your classroom?

How can you encourage leaders to use their influence for good?

Who are the leaders in your classroom?

You make an impact when you encourage your students to be leaders.

Lesson 51
Lasting Influence

There are many ways to approach standards, benchmarks, and curriculum. Your choices show students what you find important and valuable. This story comes from Venus, who remembers being inspired in Mr. Poole's class.

Mr. Poole was my high school physical education teacher. I was not into sports, and I was not looking forward to his class. But I needed to meet my physical education requirement. I soon realized that Mr. Poole didn't see his role as teaching us how to play games. Instead, he was on a mission to help us live healthier lives.

I learned so much about health and fitness from Mr. Poole. He didn't like the word diet, but he advocated for nutritious eating. He taught us that food is the fuel we need to keep our bodies going. He also wasn't a fan of extreme workouts. He helped each of us find an enjoyable and sustainable fitness plan.

I still use the information I learned in Mr. Poole's class. Thanks to him, I developed habits that have served me well. I participated in a 5k run last year, and I saw Mr. Poole at the finish line. He was cheering on his students, present and past. I'm grateful for his continued influence.

Reflection

Venus says what all teachers want to hear – "I still use the information I learned …" You likely became a teacher to make this kind of impact on students' lives. Sure, you have a responsibility to guide students into mastering standards, but there is so much more to share.

DOI: 10.4324/9781003366423-52

What inspired you to become a teacher?

What choices do you make that reveal your priorities to your students?

Which teachers had a lasting influence in your life?

You make an impact when you teach intentionally and influence students' understanding of the world.

Lesson 52
Opening Doors

It's fun to introduce your students to new things, especially when they're eager to explore new ideas and concepts. This story comes from Jaycee, who remembers thinking beyond borders in Mrs. Ray's classroom:

> I grew up in a small town, and during my childhood, I never traveled far from home. I didn't think too much about the world beyond my backyard until I encountered Mrs. Ray, my sixth-grade social studies teacher. Early in the semester, she put us in small groups and assigned each group a country. Each week, one of the groups would teach the rest of the class about their country.
>
> My group was given Italy. We created a bulletin board with a historical timeline and major landmarks. Teaching our classmates some words and phrases in Italian was both challenging and fun. Our parents even helped us provide some Italian desserts (cannoli, napoleon, and tiramisu).
>
> I looked forward to learning about a new country every week. Collecting travel brochures and dreaming about the places I wanted to visit became my favorite hobby. I've been to a dozen countries now, and I love experiencing other cultures. I am forever grateful to Mrs. Ray for showing me there is a big world to explore.

Reflection

Students depend on you to introduce them to new concepts, ideas, skills, people, and places. You have many opportunities to help them expand their understanding of the world and their

DOI: 10.4324/9781003366423-53

places in it. For many of us, this is a rewarding outcome for the work of teaching.

How do you create a class culture that values new ideas?

How do you help students open their minds to things outside of their daily lives?

What, beyond the standards, do you think your students need to learn right now?

You make an impact when you teach students to value new experiences and learning.

Lesson 53
One Caring Adult

All students have needs, and some have deep needs. There are times when you may be the only adult in a position to help. This story comes from Theo, who remembers the generosity he found in Mrs. Hudson's classroom:

> At the time I grew up (in a small farming town), our school didn't have a cafeteria or programs to provide lunch for kids. We all packed our lunches at home and carried them to school. There were many mouths to feed in my house, and there was never quite enough food to go around. So, I scraped together what I could to make myself a lunch.
>
> One day, my teacher, Mrs. Hudson, was walking around the lunch tables while we ate. She noticed that I just had a few crackers and an apple I picked off a tree on the way to school. I tried to tell her that I hadn't been feeling well and just didn't want to eat. The truth is, I was hungry. It was difficult to watch the other kids eating their lunches.
>
> The next day at lunch, Mrs. Hudson handed me a ham and cheese sandwich wrapped in waxed paper. She said she had accidentally packed two sandwiches and wondered if I would eat the extra for her. She accidentally packed two sandwiches every day for the rest of the school year. I know my teacher wasn't well off either, and I understood the sacrifice she made for me. I can't even explain my gratitude for her kindness. When I was hopelessly hungry, she fed my body and soul.

DOI: 10.4324/9781003366423-54

Reflection

There are many needs in your classroom, so you keep snacks in a drawer, write notes of encouragement, and keep school supplies on hand to share. As the caring adult in the room, you have a clear view of a student who is struggling or hurting in some way. You also have resources beyond the classroom. When you provide what students need, you help them feel safe and seen.

How do you encourage students to be open with you when they are in need?

How can you reach out to help students subtly to maintain their privacy?

Who, in your room, needs a little extra care?

You make an impact when you care about your students enough to reach out to them when they need help.

Lesson 54
Knowing and Noting

Day by day, you observe your students in ways no one else does. You understand their abilities, curiosities, idiosyncrasies, insecurities, and talents. This story comes from Ava, who remembers when her teacher, Mr. Luis, showed her he was paying attention:

> Although I'd worked hard to meet the academic expectations for scholarships, I was nervous about asking my teachers to write letters of recommendation. My guidance counselor had advised me to give my teachers plenty of time to write the letters. She also suggested I provide my teachers with some information about myself and about the scholarship requirements to help them draft the letters.
>
> My first recommendation letter came from my English teacher, Mr. Luis. He gave me an extra copy of the letter to keep. I waited until I got outside the school to read it. My teacher certainly made an effort to forge relationships with his students, but that letter was evidence of just how well he knew me. He wrote about my penchant for asking questions and my attention to detail. He even included my interest in contemporary literature authored by women of color.
>
> It was wonderful to feel known by my teacher. I respected and admired Mr. Luis, and I realized he had devoted discretionary time and attention to me. That letter meant more to me than the scholarship it helped me receive. I still have it in a box with other accolades from my high school years. It brings back sweet memories of my time with Mr. Luis, and it reminds me of the importance of making people feel seen and known.

DOI: 10.4324/9781003366423-55

Reflection

When you focus on building relationships, your students feel seen and understood. They may not realize how deeply you understand them, but they know you value them as individuals. Feeling valued allows them to take academic risks with confidence. The positive relationships you forge with your students help them build a foundation of valuing and respecting themselves.

How important is it to you to build and maintain relationships with your students?

How do you reach out to students to ensure they feel seen and valued?

What do you gain by building relationships with students?

You make an impact when you make the effort to see and know your students.

Lesson 55
Getting Uncomfortable

Students are apt to embrace the stereotypes they are assigned, but they grow when they push against those limiting expectations. This story comes from Lucas, who remembers growing through discomfort in Miss Keane's classroom:

By the time I got to high school, I'd learned to ignore my emotions. I was a football player and was taught that feeling things meant I was weak. Miss Keane taught the opposite. She encouraged me to think about the way the characters felt in the books we read, and she encouraged me to express my own emotions through my writing.

On Fridays, we read poetry. I found it both affirmative and challenging. The poems resonated with me in a way that I couldn't ignore. They also made me think about the world in new ways. We used the last half of class to write our own poems. I struggled to select a topic and to find the right words.

Miss Keane would remind me to write about what I knew. She would tell me that poetry can add magic and mystery to seemingly ordinary things. And so, I wrote about football. I found myself writing about pain, disappointment, and exhilaration. I found myself writing about pride and about shame. All of the things I pushed down came out on the paper on Fridays.

I learned to feel things again in Miss Keane's classroom. It didn't make me weak; it made me stronger. I am a better person, spouse, and parent because I allow myself to feel things. I am grateful to Miss Keane for helping me understand my emotions and teaching me to see the magic and mystery in ordinary things.

DOI: 10.4324/9781003366423-56

Reflection

When you create a classroom environment where struggle is embraced, you help students engage in new practices. Learners meet the expectations of their teachers. When you believe in them, they begin to believe in themselves.

What could your students learn by trying something new?

What messages about stretching their minds are your students learning in your classroom?

How do you encourage students to embrace the discomfort of learning and growing in new ways?

You make an impact when you give students opportunities to embrace the struggle of growing in a new direction.

Lesson 56
Instilling Pride

You never know which strategy or lesson is going to hook which student. But, if you are lucky, some of your students will reach back to you as they mature to let you know how something in your classroom inspired them. This story comes from Cassie, who remembers how Mrs. Gibbs motivated her for life:

I walked into my kindergarten classroom and immediately noticed my name (the one word I could read) written on my desk, my cubby, and my coat hook. I soon learned to write my name, and because the names of classmates were so prominently displayed, I learned to write my friends' names, too. I wrote our names in paint on big pieces of paper and on sidewalks with big pieces of chalk. I was so proud when I wrote my classmates' names on each of their Valentine cards and signed each card myself.

One spring day, we wrote our names on big, Styrofoam cups. We filled each cup with rich, brown soil and carefully added a bean seed. Mrs. Gibbs lined the cups up in the windowsill. Every morning, I ran into the classroom to find the cup with my name. It seemed like forever, but one day I peeked in to find a tiny sprout. I still remember that cup with my name on the outside and a tall, green bean plant growing inside.

Mrs. Gibbs filled my kindergarten days with play and projects, and she taught me to proudly put my name on my work. I was always so excited to bring home a painting, a paper, or a bean plant with my name written on it. Even now, I try to make sure the work I do is worthy of my name.

DOI: 10.4324/9781003366423-57

Reflection

When you intentionally create a classroom culture that helps students feel proud of their accomplishments, they develop competence and confidence. Each day, you provide opportunities for your students to take pride in themselves as learners. You are the sun in your classroom, encouraging your learners to grow.

What are your beliefs about your students and their abilities?

What would you like your students to carry with them as they leave your class?

How do you build a culture of academic pride in your classroom?

You make an impact when you give students opportunities to become lifelong learners.

Lesson 57
Being Tenacious

It's our job to meet students where they are and move them forward. There are times when growth requires relentless focus from you and your students. This story comes from Nicolas, who remembers growing in Mrs. Alfonso's classroom:

My family moved to Florida from Costa Rica when I was in middle school. It was a difficult adjustment. My English was limited when I arrived, but by the time I got to high school, I was a fluent English speaker. I was not a great writer though.

I met Mrs. Alfonso at the beginning of my freshman year. She was a resource teacher for students who spoke English as a second language. When we met for the first time, she explained that I was doing well in math but needed support in English class. I soon learned that her way of supporting closely resembled that of my soccer coach – intense and unrelenting. I still remember what she said to me: "You are smart, Nicolas, but people will not see how smart you are if you can't write proficiently. It will limit your opportunities." She insisted that I give her my papers before I turned them in. She had this purple pen, and my papers would end up a sea of purple. She didn't just mark them; she went over every correction with me. That's right. *Every. Single. Correction.*

When I graduated from high school, I was a better writer than most of my native English-speaking friends. I did well in my college English classes and eventually made it into law school. Writing and speaking are indispensable parts of a lawyer's work. I know that Mrs. Alfonso was right: my credibility and my confidence would have been hindered by my limitations. I always knew that she loved me, in a tenacious purple-pen-wielding kind of way.

DOI: 10.4324/9781003366423-58

Reflection

Everything in your classroom is designed to move your students past their limitations (real or perceived) – every lesson, strategy, and assignment. Relentless focus on growth requires tenacity. You are your students' guide and cheerleader, and they need your unwavering support, whatever shape it takes.

How will your students' daily efforts in class carry into their futures?

How are you intentional with your persistence?

What helps you replenish your determined spirit after a long day?

You make an impact when you are tenacious in your teachings.

Lesson 58
Making Magic

Sometimes your students really get it, and what they've been struggling to understand finally clicks. Those moments are enchanting for you and for them. This story comes from Liam, who remembers Mr. Charles' captivating lessons:

I don't remember being particularly curious as a young kid. I was very active, and it was difficult to sit still for instruction in the classroom. But my fifth-grade teacher, Mr. Charles, had a way of sparking my curiosity. He would do a magic trick every Friday morning, but he wouldn't tell us how the trick worked until right before dismissal. We would try to guess the secret all day.

I remember the day he put a skewer through a balloon without popping or deflating it. I could hardly wait until the secret was revealed that afternoon. Mr. Charles explained how balloons are made of long chains of molecules called polymers. The elasticity of the polymers allows the balloon to stretch. The polymer chains of the balloon close around the skewer which stops the air escaping and allows it to stay inflated.

My teacher's explanations always centered around science concepts. I became fascinated with science and often recreated the magic tricks at home. Learning the tricks also improved my focus, as I had to keep working at them to perform them successfully. I even made some money during high school by doing magic shows at kids' birthday parties. And, in honor of Mr. Charles, I always integrated some science concepts. I'm grateful for the way he sparked my curiosity and created magic in the classroom.

DOI: 10.4324/9781003366423-59

Reflection

For many students, school has a magical quality. It is where the secrets of life are revealed, and you are the magician who unveils it all. Great teaching often looks like sleight of hand, but it is actually careful planning, preparation, and a big bag of tricks. Magic doesn't happen every day, but when it does – voila!

What do your students want and need to learn?

What are your go-to strategies for engagement?

Who is your role model for the magic of teaching?

You make an impact when you spend time planning to allow magic to happen.

Lesson 59
Instructing Implicitly

You may be asked to implement a social emotional curriculum, but it's most effective when it connects with students' learning and their lives. This story comes from Lydia, who remembers the important lessons just outside Mrs. August's classroom:

> I was a highly anxious kid, and my anxiety got worse as I progressed through high school. I worried about everything, and I often suffered from headaches. But I found some relief in an unexpected place. In the fall of my senior year, I ended up in Mrs. August's environmental science class. Her passion for birds was evident in the posters on the walls and collection of guidebooks on the shelves.
>
> Every Friday, Mrs. August took us birdwatching in the park next to our school. Armed with binoculars and spiral notebooks, we would move quietly around the trees looking for different species of birds. At first, I just thought it was fun to get outside, but focusing on spotting and identifying the birds kept me from focusing on my worries. I found listening to the birds soothing, too. I started to go birdwatching in the evenings, and I noticed that my headaches lessened.
>
> Now I realize that Mrs. August wasn't just teaching me about birds; she was teaching me about mindfulness. In addition to learning much about bird behavior, I learned about the power of being fully present. Learning to quiet my mind and focus on my surroundings is a lesson that has continued to enrich my life.

DOI: 10.4324/9781003366423-60

Reflection

Everyone can use some peaceful moments in the day. When you build them into your class plans, you also get the benefits of mid-day mindfulness. You promote well-being when you show your students how to care for themselves, especially when you model it.

What helps you focus and let go of worries?

How can you teach your students the importance of mindfulness and relaxation?

Who in your classroom is struggling with anxiety or stress?

You make an impact when you model the importance of mental and emotional health.

Lesson 60
Striking a Spark

You never know when a spark of interest will become a flame in your classroom, but it's rewarding to watch it happen. This story comes from Leo, who remembers an eye-opening lesson in Mr. Segal's classroom:

> Growing up, I never read just for pleasure, except for comic books. The summer before eleventh grade, I managed to complete my summer reading assignment with considerable pressure from my mom. It was *The Odyssey*, and I had a hard time following the story.
>
> When I got to Mr. Segal's class in the fall, I was ready for the usual comprehension quizzes, but he had a different plan. Mr. Segal taught us about the Hero's Journey. He said it was a journey taken by many fictional characters, even Luke Skywalker in *Star Wars*. He discussed our summer reading book through that framework and explained how Odysseus went through the stages of the Hero's Journey from hearing the call to becoming the master of his fate.
>
> I started to see the stages of the journey everywhere, even in my superhero comics. Mr. Segal recommended other books in which the main character followed the Hero's Journey. It was the spark that led to my love of reading. Thanks to Mr. Segal, I always have a stack of books on my bedside table.

Reflection

Sometimes you get to witness a lightbulb moment, when a student experiences a sudden understanding. Though you see it start, you may never realize how far that fire of new knowledge

DOI: 10.4324/9781003366423-61

spreads. Be assured, it lasts long after students leave your classroom.

How can you capitalize on a student's spark of understanding?

How do you encourage students once you realize they've gotten it?

What can you do to help students who are still struggling to find their lightbulb?

You make an impact when you light the fire to learn in your students.

Lesson 61
Reinforcing Positively

Classroom management is significant for all teachers. It is likely the least fun, but a vital part of school for both you and your students. This story comes from Brock, who remembers Mrs. Crew's innovative approach to creating order in her classroom:

> I always appreciated teachers who could add some fun to an ordinary day. My seventh-grade pre-algebra teacher, Mrs. Crew, was one of those teachers. She had a special way of rewarding us for extra effort or for helping her. When we went above and beyond, we could earn Crewpons (like coupons, only cooler).
>
> I organized the books on Mrs. Crew's shelf one day and earned a Crewpon to sit in the rolling chair. When I did especially well on a quiz, I earned a Crewpon to wear a hat in class for one period. She had so many different rewards printed on them, from homework reduction to an opportunity to add a song to the class playlist.
>
> Even though we tried to be cool, all the students loved earning a Crewpon. It wasn't really the reward printed on the Crewpon that mattered; the reward was typically a small and somewhat silly thing. It was the recognition of effort and the fun of seeing the creative things Mrs. Crew came up with. Many of my other classes were structured around lists of rules and consequences for not adhering to them, but Mrs. Crew found a way to put a positive and amusing spin on classroom management.

DOI: 10.4324/9781003366423-62

Reflection

Managing behaviors can seem like a momentous challenge, and you have likely tried many strategies. Students respond to creative approaches, and the happier they are, the more cooperative they will be. When you add a little fun to your management plan, everyone wins.

How do you like to be managed?

How do your students respond to positive reinforcement versus negative reinforcement?

What can you do to bring more positivity into your classroom management?

You make an impact when you find ways to highlight the good you see in your students.

Lesson 62
Going Big

Your daily lessons are focused on benchmarks and goals. Sometimes, though, you want to have fun with your students as they learn. This story comes from Randy, who remembers a whole month of lessons in Mrs. McGee's classroom:

> I was in fifth grade in 1984, the year of the Winter Olympics in Sarajevo. Our teacher, Mrs. McGee, organized the whole month of February around an Olympics theme. I remember it so clearly. There were several competitions from speed problem-solving in math to cross-country reading. Speed problem-solving was a team sport. A problem was placed on the overhead projector, and the first team to find the correct answer earned a point. At the end of the competition, the team with the most total points won the gold medal. Cross-country reading involved reading from a list of books representing different cultures around the world. When students completed each book and the associated quiz, they earned points.
>
> I was so excited to come to school during those weeks; I didn't even realize I was learning. Mrs. McGee did incorporate some things just for fun. She put a cassette of classical music on the tape player, and we "ice skated" around the room in our socks. She brought in small white pom poms made from yarn, and we had snowball fights. The culminating event was a medal ceremony. I'm not sure where our teacher got medals, but everyone earned one. We took turns standing on the podium (a wooden step stool) while the National Anthem played. Thinking back to this time, I'm in awe of Mrs. McGee's creativity. She managed to teach basic skills, build teamwork, and

DOI: 10.4324/9781003366423-63

cultivate a sense of pride all in a month full of fun and excitement. And I think she enjoyed it almost as much as we did.

Reflection

Mrs. McGee absolutely enjoyed this memorable month as much as her students did. It takes a lot of planning to create a month of themed lessons and engaging activities. You deserve to have fun with your students and find joy in your work. And a little fun can lead to big learning.

How can you start small with a theme that will engage your students while they learn?

How would your students respond to some well-planned fun during their learning day?

Who can you turn to for inspiration or collaboration?

You make an impact when you have fun with your students as they learn.

Lesson 63
Helping Students Connect

Some of your students struggle to find their place at school. It can be rewarding when you bring like minds together, creating a welcoming space for your students. This story comes from Becky, who remembers finding a group of her own in Mr. Crandall's classroom:

> By eighth grade, my peers had divided themselves into three main groups. One group was the athletes, and another group was artistic. I admired both groups, but I definitely did not have athletic or artistic tendencies. The third group consisted of kids who were passionate about fashion and were heavily invested in the social scene. I was an introvert who wore old jeans and rotated through the same five T-shirts every week. I just didn't fit in anywhere.
>
> In the fall of my eighth-grade year, a new teacher came to our school. Mr. Crandall taught social studies, and one day, he announced that he was starting an after-school chess club. I didn't know anything about chess, but it piqued my interest. About a dozen students signed up, and Mr. Crandall spent the first few meetings teaching us the fundamentals. He taught us to number the rows (ranks) on the board from 1 to and 8 and identify the columns (files) with the letters A to H. Then he taught us basic moves using the coordinates.
>
> Chess just clicked for me, and I became obsessed with learning different moves and mastering the game. Mr. Crandall left the boards and pieces set up on a table in the back of his classroom. A few other students and I started playing during lunch. I felt like I found my group. Many

DOI: 10.4324/9781003366423-64

of those chess club members remained close friends through high school and beyond. I'm grateful that Mr. Crandall helped me find my passion and my people.

Reflection

It is hard to see your students struggle socially. As a compassionate teacher who pays attention to all aspects of a student's development, you see who is having trouble finding their place in your class and in the larger social structure of the school. When you bring like students together for a purpose, lasting friendships can begin.

Who in your classroom is still looking for their place in the social life of school?

Who can you bring together due to shared interests or quirks?

What strategies do you use to bring students together?

You make an impact when you help your students connect with new friends.

Lesson 64
Teaching Self-Advocacy

All students are entitled to quality education, but in order to access it, they must learn to ask for what they need. Self-advocacy is an important skill. This story comes from Farrah, who remembers Mrs. Baylor's powerful lesson:

> I was a timid child, and I was always reluctant to ask my teachers for help. I felt like I was bothering them. When I found myself struggling in geometry class during the fall of my sophomore year, I knew my only option was to seek help from my teacher. I had exhausted all other resources in trying to complete a homework assignment, so I mustered up all my courage and stopped by to see my teacher after school.
>
> I remember softly knocking on Mrs. Baylor's door and peeking inside. She cheerfully waved me in and invited me to sit in a chair by her desk. I apologized profusely for bothering her. She stopped me and (in a voice much sterner than usual) told me never to apologize for asking for what I needed.
>
> It was a message I would hear from Mrs. Baylor over and over. Every time I started to apologize for asking a question, she would put up her hand and remind me that I have a right to advocate for myself and my own learning. It was one of the most powerful lessons I learned in all my years of schooling. Thanks to Mrs. Baylor, I stopped shrinking back and started speaking up.

DOI: 10.4324/9781003366423-65

Reflection

It is never too early to encourage your students to advocate for themselves. When you teach them how to request what they need and speak for themselves, you help build confident young people who are ready to face challenges. Your own transparency about advocating for yourself and your school community is a great way to model this behavior.

How do your students seek to have their needs met?

How do you teach your students about their rights within the school and society?

What are the self-advocacy behaviors you want to see from your students?

You make an impact when you help students find and use their voices.

Lesson 65
Breaking Barriers

Though they love to think outside the box, students often get stuck in old assumptions. Your classroom can open a new world to your students. This story comes from Jessinia, who remembers an eye-opening lesson in Ms. Carter's classroom:

> When I got my schedule on the first day of tenth grade, I noticed that my second-period class was Biology with a new teacher named Carter. I walked into class expecting to see Mr. Carter. I was surprised to be greeted at the door by Ms. Carter, a young woman of color.
>
> Soon after the bell rang, Ms. Carter passed out blank sheets of paper and asked us to draw a scientist. Most of us drew older men with crazy hair and glasses, like Einstein. Ms. Carter followed that exercise with a series of slides showing acclaimed scientists of many different racial, ethnic, and gender identities. My mind was blown.
>
> As a young woman of color myself, I had never even considered a career in the sciences. Ms. Carter became an important mentor and advocate for me. She helped me get into college where I majored in organic chemistry. I eventually earned my PhD, and now I try to pay it forward by encouraging other young women to consider paths they never believed were possible.

Reflection

Your students need you to help expand their thinking with new ideas and information. By challenging assumptions and limiting paradigms, you help change their worldviews and how they see themselves within the larger picture. You may even inspire your students to see new options for their futures.

DOI: 10.4324/9781003366423-66

What do you bring to class to help your students see the world and themselves differently?

What paradigms would you like to see shift in your community?

How can you help your students expand their thinking?

You make an impact when you show your students a new world of possibilities.

Lesson 66
Inspiring Pride

You are adept at seeing what your students need and helping them find it. Sometimes you step outside the curriculum to do it, but an inspiring lesson or task can be life-changing. This story comes from Jamal, who remembers finding beauty in Mrs. Branch's classroom:

> I grew up in a tough neighborhood on the south side of Chicago. There weren't many flowers, mostly cracked concrete sidewalks and buildings in need of repair. Until my junior year in high school, I would have said there wasn't much beauty where I lived. Lucky for me, Mrs. Branch opened my eyes.
>
> Mrs. Branch was my English teacher, and somehow, she got funding to purchase several digital cameras for our class. She let us check out the cameras under one condition – we had to capture images of beautiful things in our neighborhood. It's funny how looking for beautiful things helped me see the beauty around me that I hadn't noticed before.
>
> When we returned the cameras, Mrs. Branch printed many of our pictures and put them in a collage on a bulletin board. There were pictures of colorful fruit in the market, paintings sprayed by graffiti artists in the subway, and kids splashing in an open fire hydrant. Standing back to take it all in, I suddenly felt proud of my roots. I am forever grateful to Mrs. Branch for helping me learn to look for beauty wherever I am.

DOI: 10.4324/9781003366423-67

Reflection

Jamal's memory is a reminder that we must see through our students' eyes before we can ask them to look at things differently. Your students may deal with some difficult situations and real struggles. They need you to help open their eyes to what is beautiful. As you help your students see the good around them, they will also see the good within them.

What do you see when you look around through students' eyes?

What are some inspiring and special things in your school's community?

How can you help your students see good things reflected in themselves?

You make an impact when you inspire students' pride in their community and themselves.

Lesson 67
Guiding and Providing

You plant seeds of confidence in your students each day and water them in praise and positive reinforcement. Your students know you believe in them, which helps them believe in themselves. This story comes from Mateo, who remembers growing with Mrs. Hardin's guidance:

> I was in fifth grade and several grade levels behind in reading. I was frustrated and embarrassed. One day, my homeroom teacher told me that I was going to spend my reading block helping the second-grade teacher, Mrs. Hardin. When I walked into her classroom the first time, Mrs. Hardin introduced me as the special reading tutor.
>
> She always had a seat ready for me at the reading table where she worked with small groups. I would help hand out the sticky notes and highlighters, and she always made sure there was an extra book for me to follow along in case one of the younger ones needed assistance. I must admit, it was a brilliant plan. Before I knew it, my reading was improving.
>
> I loved being in Mrs. Hardin's classroom. She never made me feel like a failure. Instead, she treated me like an asset, and the second graders looked up to me. My competence and my confidence grew. I got a beautiful letter from Mrs. Hardin when I graduated from high school. In her letter, she thanked me for helping her and for being a model of persistence for her students.

DOI: 10.4324/9781003366423-68

Reflection

When your students struggle, their confidence dips. Even students who are successful in many ways start to question themselves when something is difficult. But you understand that success lies on the other side, and your support helps them reach their goals. As their competence grows, so does their confidence.

How do you know when a student is struggling with low confidence?

How is confidence building part of your class culture?

Who in your class needs a confidence boost today?

You make an impact by building students up when their confidence is low.

Lesson 68
Inspiring Adventure

At times, you may be the only one who understands your students' dreams (or the only one in a position to encourage them). This story comes from Liza, who remembers being inspired in Mr. Finney's classroom:

I grew up in the middle of the Midwest, but in my dreams, I was a mermaid. I was obsessed with everything about the ocean, and I longed to visit the beach. My third-grade teacher, Mr. Finney, was from the California coast, and I would beg him to tell me stories about surfing and snorkeling.

Over our winter break, Mr. Finney returned home to visit his family. When he came back to school, he gave each of his students a baggie with a small amount of sand and a shell. He told us about his long walks on the shore, picking out just the perfect shell for each of us. I think I may have even slept with that baggie under my pillow.

Mr. Finney continued to be an important person in my life, and he always brought back items from the shore for me when he went back home. Now I have visited beaches all over the world, and my favorite thing to do on my travels is find the perfect shell to drop in the mail with a letter to Mr. Finney.

Reflection

All students have dreams. Even when they are not realistic, you can help students see the possibilities. You can help them create plans and encourage them to keep dreaming. It is important that your students know you are on their dream team.

DOI: 10.4324/9781003366423-69

How do you discover your students' dreams for the future?

How does your class culture support the dreams of each student?

What do you do to help your students create realistic plans to achieve their dreams?

You make an impact when you believe in and encourage your students' dreams.

Lesson 69
Opening Doors

It is easy to see when a student starts changing, but sometimes hard to know why. Often, a student needs an adult who cares enough to ask what's going on. This story comes from Yolanda, who remembers an important conversation outside Mr. Kress' classroom door:

> Right before my fifteenth birthday, my father moved to another state. I was really angry, but I didn't know how to deal with my feelings. Even the smallest frustration sent me over the edge. I lost patience with everyone, even the people I loved. I treated my mother and brother disrespectfully, and I constantly argued with my friends.
>
> One day a boy in my history class was kicking the back of my chair. He was just playing around, but I reacted by shouting and knocking the books off his desk. My teacher, Mr. Kress, walked out into the hall with me. He said he was worried about me, and I told him about my father. My teacher (also the cross-country coach) shared how he found running helpful for managing his emotions, and he invited me to try running with his team.
>
> From that very first practice, running brought me a sense of calm. Mr. Kress once explained that running increases dopamine and serotonin, but I just knew it made me feel better. I was headed down a destructive path, but my teacher helped me find a constructive way to deal with my emotions.

DOI: 10.4324/9781003366423-70

Reflection

There are times you need to step outside the hum of your classroom to intervene in a student's day. You know how to ask the right questions and when to push a little or back off. What matters most is that you open the door to conversation about your student's needs. Once you understand the situation, you can help.

What are the signs you look for when your students are changing?

What do you do when your students seem to need a one-on-one conversation?

How are you an encourager to your students?

You make an impact when you notice your students need someone to open the door to important conversations.

Lesson 70
Inspiring Connections

As a teacher, you want more for your students than mastering the curriculum. You are preparing your students for life, and all the stressful and wonderful things ahead. This story comes from Johanna, who remembers an activity in Ms. Currie's classroom that changed her way of thinking:

> I'm definitely introverted, and the thought of mingling has always made me anxious. My high school speech teacher, Ms. Currie, had a fun way of helping me develop useful strategies and become more comfortable in social situations. At the start of every class, we spent a few minutes in Speed Debating, kind of like speed dating but without the risk of rejection.
>
> Ms. Currie would give us a topic, like whether dogs or cats make better pets. She then played music, and when the music stopped, we debated the topic with the person closest to us for three minutes. When the music started again, we moved to a new partner. It was an easy and fun way to get to know people.
>
> Now, whenever I have to go to a party or networking event, I just pretend it's Speed Debating. I find a person nearby and throw out a topic, like pancakes versus waffles. The other person always looks both amused and relieved. I'm forever grateful to Ms. Currie for teaching me how to turn what was once a source of anxiety into an enjoyable experience.

DOI: 10.4324/9781003366423-71

Reflection

Your classroom is a microcosm of the world, full of different personalities and perspectives. When you create experiences for your students that help them navigate the big world, they are better prepared. The things they are learning will serve them well beyond your classroom.

What do you hope your students remember from their year with you?

How do you thread life skills into your class procedures, activities, and lessons?

What are the life skills you want your students to master this year?

You make an impact when you nurture your students' growth as people as well as learners.

Lesson 71
Giving Resources

Your students don't know what they don't know – yet. One of the rewards of teaching is the opportunity to introduce students to a resource they can use throughout their lives. This story comes from Ranal, who remembers a field trip with Mrs. Dunn's class:

As a young child, I loved reading, but we didn't have many books at home. I'm sure that's why I have this very clear memory of going on a field trip to the public library when I was in second grade. My teacher, Mrs. Dunn, had prepared us for the trip by teaching us about the Dewey Decimal System and how to use the card catalogue. She also made sure we completed applications to get our own library cards.

I remember the sense of awe as I walked into the library; I'd never seen so many books. Practically running to the children's section, I took a book about baseball off the shelf, flipped through the pages, looked at the pictures, and tried reading the words. Once I had chosen two books, Mrs. Dunn helped me get my library card and check out my books. I could hardly believe I got to take the books home.

I read those books every night until my mother took me back to the library to turn them in and check out new ones. That trip was the beginning of a love affair with the library. Even now, when I can purchase books online or at a bookstore, I still love to check them out from my neighborhood library. And every time I pull out my library card, I think of Mrs. Dunn.

DOI: 10.4324/9781003366423-72

Reflection

Ranal's story reveals the way seemingly ordinary things can be revelations to our students. There are likely things you don't even remember learning (though someone introduced you to them). No matter the socio-economic make-up of your school, your students still need the resources you can provide.

What resources did you learn about when you were your students' age?

What can you do to enlighten your students about what is available to them?

When would be the perfect time to either bring your students to the community or your community to them?

You make an impact when you leverage resources to introduce students to new things.

Lesson 72
Providing Opportunity

Our students may not always do the right things for the right reasons, but that is okay. A first step can begin a lifelong walk. This story comes from Mark, who remembers learning about serving his community with Mrs. Hadley's club:

At the beginning of my junior year in high school, I joined a service club because I thought it would look good on my college applications. I was looking forward to socializing but not so excited about the community service requirement. Our club advisor, Mrs. Hadley, announced that our first service opportunity was to assist with the Special Olympics event happening nearby. There were several jobs needing to be filled, and I chose to be the timekeeper for the running competitions.

When we climbed into the van on the morning of the event, I was tired and cranky. But my attitude changed quickly once we arrived. I was inspired by the enthusiasm and persistence of the athletes. Despite their challenges, they never complained. As the competitions began, I found myself cheering so loudly that I had no voice by the end of the day.

On the ride back to school, Mrs. Hadley asked us to reflect on what we had given and what we had gained through our service that day. I'd never thought about community service as a mutually beneficial activity before. I realized the Special Olympians had given me a day full of inspiration and joy, and all it cost me was operating the stopwatch. I'm grateful to my teacher for that lesson and for inspiring my continuing commitment to serving my community.

DOI: 10.4324/9781003366423-73

Reflection

It makes sense that students want to know why they are doing something and what is in it for them before they commit. After all, adults do, too. You can help students stretch by offering many and varied opportunities to try new things, even when they are initially reluctant.

What types of activities inspire you to be a more engaged member of your community?

What opportunities do you bring to your students to help them learn about themselves through service?

How can you inspire your students to give to others without looking for reward?

You make an impact when you inspire students to serve, whether in big or small ways.

Lesson 73
Nurturing Talent

Young adults may be surprised to learn about multiple intelligences. Somehow, many get the message that there's only one way to be smart. Helping them see different types of strengths and abilities can be life-changing. This story comes from Leo, who remembers Mrs. Grant's classroom, where his strength was celebrated:

> I was never a particularly good student. I struggled to sit still, and I was always taking my pen apart or messing with the paper clips I found. I liked to tinker with things, and I never felt like I belonged in school, except in Mrs. Grant's fifth-grade class.
>
> Back then, when our teacher wanted to show a movie, she rolled out a projector that lit the film onto the screen as it moved from one reel to the other. When Mrs. Grant's projector suddenly stopped working in the middle of a movie one day, everyone groaned in disappointment. I asked her if I could try to fix it, and she told me to give it a go. As the rest of the class moved on to math, I took that projector apart, cleaned off some of the pieces, and put it back together. When it worked again, I was hailed as a hero.
>
> I became the fixer of all broken things in Mrs. Grant's classroom, from the pencil sharpener to the record player. It gave me a sense of pride and purpose. Other teachers saw my fidgeting as a nuisance, but Mrs. Grant recognized my strength. I am forever grateful to her for helping me feel a sense of belonging while also appreciating my unique gifts.

DOI: 10.4324/9781003366423-74

Reflection

Your students want to be seen and appreciated, just like everyone else. When you can tap into each student's individual talent and type of intelligence, you create an environment where everyone feels appreciated. More importantly, when you create an environment where all students feel successful, you have a room full of scholars ready to take academic risks together.

Who may be feeling different in your classroom right now?

Who can be inspired by capitalizing on their individual talents?

What are the benefits of praising students who are productive in an atypical way?

You make an impact when you truly see your students and celebrate them for their differences.

Lesson 74
Impacting Their Futures

Inspired teachers create sparks. When you are excited about what you are teaching and who you are teaching, your passion shows, and it spreads. This story comes from Gianna, who remembers being inspired in Mr. Catania's classroom:

> I took an anatomy class in high school because it fit into my schedule. I couldn't have predicted then that it would inspire my life's work. I remember walking into Mr. Catania's classroom on the first day and noticing the walls covered with charts and the tables covered with models of bones and organs. Before that class, I'd hardly thought about the complexity of my body or even how it worked.
>
> Mr. Catania was passionate about teaching, and after every unit on a different system of the body, he would remind us that we are beautifully and miraculously made. Because of his class, I began to appreciate and care for my body differently. I understood the importance of drinking water, eating healthy foods, and staying away from drugs. When I broke my arm playing soccer, I brought Mr. Catania my X-ray, and he spent a whole class period explaining how my arm would heal.
>
> Mr. Catania's passion was contagious, and I found myself fascinated with anatomy, too. After high school, I decided to study nursing. Now I work in pediatrics, and I love helping kids understand how their bodies work and the miraculous ways they heal. I am grateful to Mr. Catania for sparking this passion and for inspiring me to choose a career in which I can make an impact on others, just as he did for me.

DOI: 10.4324/9781003366423-75

Reflection

Gianna's memory is a reminder of how often students look to their teachers for inspiration. When you are passionate and inspired about what you are teaching, your students are passionate and inspired about learning. The impact you are making may be hard to recognize at times, but you have already led students to new interests, paths of studies, and even career plans.

What lessons or units inspire you to be the best teacher you can be?

Why are these your favorite things to share with your students?

How can you capitalize on the energy in your classroom during your most inspired teaching?

You make an impact when you share your passion and create sparks in the classroom.

Lesson 75
Finding Strengths

Though students are accustomed to their peers moving in and out of groups and classrooms, receiving accommodations, it can feel different when it's their turn. Your support can turn a challenge into an opportunity for growth. This story comes from James, who remembers finding his strength in Mrs. King's classroom:

> I had a difficult time learning to read, and I had fallen far behind my peers by the time I reached fifth grade. Instead of staying with the rest of my class during reading, I began going to another room to work with Mrs. King. I was embarrassed and felt like there must be something wrong with me. I decided I just wasn't as smart as the other kids.
>
> I remember walking into Mrs. King's room on that first day. The walls of her small room were covered with pictures of famous people. There was Walt Disney, Albert Einstein, John Lennon, and Steven Spielberg. She told me that all of them had something called dyslexia, and they had all struggled with reading when they were young. I couldn't believe these super smart people had the same challenge as me.
>
> With a great deal of patience and skill, Mrs. King helped me become a reader. The most important thing she did was help me believe in myself. She taught me that smart people can still struggle with reading. She showed me how to leverage my other strengths and persist. I am forever grateful to Mrs. King for giving me a strong foundation in reading and in life.

DOI: 10.4324/9781003366423-76

Reflection

Educators have a special way of framing challenges as stepping stones. You are uniquely positioned to give your students tools to overcome obstacles as they arise. You give your students a precious gift each time you help them build confidence and new skills.

How do you encourage students who are feeling a sense of otherness?

How does your class culture encourage students to nurture each other through challenges?

When do you intervene to help a student face an obstacle?

You make an impact when you give students tools to help them find their strengths in moments of struggle.

Lesson 76
Discovering a Passion

School can be an opportune venue for trying on activities to see what fits. This story comes from Zane, who remembers the way Mrs. Ledbetter helped him discover his passion:

Many people spend decades searching for their passion, but I found mine in third grade. I still remember the day Mrs. Ledbetter announced that our class would be putting on a play. We would perform *City Mouse, Country Mouse* for the younger students. We could sign up to try out for parts or to design scenery or costumes. I was thrilled when I got the part of City Mouse.

We rehearsed for weeks, and my sister helped me practice my lines at home. On the day of the show, Mrs. Ledbetter carefully drew on my whiskers with eyeliner and adjusted my ears. When the curtain opened, everyone in the audience cheered. I loved every minute of the performance, and I especially loved the applause at the end. I was hooked. From that day forward, I spent all my time either writing plays or acting in them.

Mrs. Ledbetter involved everyone in the class in our production of *City Mouse, Country Mouse*. I loved the teamwork from the artistic kids who designed the scenery to the kids who hustled to get the right props on the stage. Even the rehearsals were fun, as we found plenty of opportunities to laugh and be silly. I am so grateful to Mrs. Ledbetter for helping me find my passion and for showing me what it means to work in collaboration with others.

DOI: 10.4324/9781003366423-77

Reflection

In our society, where athletics are so highly respected, it can be difficult for kids who don't fit that mold. All kids need to learn about teamwork, and everyone should have the opportunity to shine. You can encourage your students by finding a way to incorporate this synergy in the classroom and finding ways to help all students shine.

How can you offer a variety of experiences to help students find the activities that spark their passions?

How can you celebrate individuality while still cultivating collaboration and synergy?

What is the value of teamwork in the classroom and beyond?

You make an impact when you help students discover their passions.

Lesson 77
Teaching More

Your professional life is full of curriculum- and lesson-planning, classroom management, and the daily bustle of school life. All of these can make it hard to see some of the most important lessons embedded in your work with students. This story comes from Alan, who remembers learning more than woodworking in Mr. Horner's classroom:

I took a woodworking class in high school. I expected to learn about saws and sandpaper, but I didn't expect the many lessons my teacher, Mr. Horner, would teach me about life. In addition to my ability to carve out a perfect notch for a hinge, I also learned about precision, patience, and pride.

Mr. Horner had all these sayings like, "Measure twice, cut once." And whenever I work on anything, I can still hear his words, "Make it worthy of putting your name on it." But mostly I remember his perspective on mistakes. Every time we completed a project, he asked us to reflect on what went wrong, and most importantly, what we learned from what went wrong.

I think about that lesson every time I make a mess, whether that mess is in a work project or a relationship. Considering my mistakes and how I can learn from them help me to not repeat them. It still amazes me how much I learned in that woodworking class and how much Mr. Horner's lessons continue to impact my life.

DOI: 10.4324/9781003366423-78

Reflection

Everything that happens in your classroom is rooted in your mindset. Your students are watching and listening to how you handle setbacks, problems, success, and even surprises. Your philosophies and general outlook can teach your students a new way to approach things. These are the little extras you teach your students every day, and these lessons can have a big impact.

What do you want to teach your students that they can carry through their entire lives?

What impact do you hope to have on your students' lives?

How are you intentional about teaching more than curriculum?

You make an impact when you inspire students through all you have taught them.

Lesson 78
Taking Time

In a busy school day, there seems to never be enough time. You are probably very good at maximizing every minute – the more you do in the building, the less you do at home! Nevertheless, you take the time to pause when a student needs you. This story comes from Cole, who remembers the time Mrs. Simpkins spent with him when he really needed her:

When I was in middle school, I got my feelings hurt easily. I always assumed someone was trying to frustrate me or exclude me. But my language arts teacher, Mrs. Simpkins, helped me think differently about the intentions of others. Whenever I got upset, she would ask me to think about what I knew for sure and what I was assuming.

I remember coming into her class one day angry because a girl I liked had ignored me in the hallway. As usual, Mrs. Simpkins asked what I knew for sure, which was only that the girl didn't respond when I walked by and said hello. Then she asked me to think of all the possibilities. Maybe this girl didn't like me, but maybe there was some other reason. Perhaps she didn't hear me or was upset about something that happened at home.

It turns out Mrs. Simpkins was right because I am now married to that girl. I am a better person, and I have better relationships thanks to my practice of questioning my assumptions. Knowing I can never really know the intentions of others allows me to give everyone the benefit of the doubt and frees me from constantly dealing with unwanted emotions. I'm grateful to Mrs. Simpkins for taking the time to have life-shaping conversations with me.

DOI: 10.4324/9781003366423-79

Reflection

A bit of objective reasoning at the right time can help your students reset. It's usually easy for you to understand what they are going through, as a person with life experience and a bird's-eye view. When you take the time to coach your students through a hard time or a misunderstanding, you help them build the cornerstones of character. It's time well spent.

Who have you noticed is struggling with the same issues again and again?

How do you reach out to students who need some non-academic coaching?

How do you encourage your students to practice what they are learning?

You make an impact when you take the time to work with students when they are having a hard time.

Lesson 79
Encouraging Confidence

It's the hope of every parent and teacher that our young people will live with confidence, never making choices out of fear. Sometimes, you may run into a student who isn't confident yet but can get there with some encouragement. This story comes from Sasha, who remembers the first seeds of self-confidence planted in Mrs. Peck's classroom:

> I was a very shy and insecure teenager. I avoided anything that seemed risky or might invite criticism. I remember a day in eighth grade when my homeroom was electing student council representatives. My friend nominated me, and I immediately asked to withdraw my name. My teacher, Mrs. Peck, suggested I think about it first.
>
> When the other kids left for lunch, Mrs. Peck asked me to stay behind and talk. She inquired about why I wanted to withdraw from the election, but I didn't have a good reason. She gently suggested that I might be rejecting myself before anybody else could reject me, and she convinced me to take a chance. When the students in my homeroom voted, I was elected to be their student council representative. It was a turning point in my life.
>
> I think about Mrs. Peck every time I find myself avoiding an opportunity. I ask myself whether I really don't want the opportunity or just don't want to risk rejection. My teacher inspired me to be brave and being brave made me more confident. She truly helped lay the foundation for my future success.

DOI: 10.4324/9781003366423-80

Reflection

You see the true potential in each of your students. There is much you can do to encourage them as they develop toward that potential. Your encouragement to try something you know they can do, to spread their wings, to see themselves as they truly are, is invaluable.

How can building their confidence help your students in and outside of class?

How do you inspire your students when they need it?

Who in your class needs some encouragement right now?

You make an impact when you care enough to help your students build confidence.

Lesson 80
Cultivating Empowering Thoughts

Teachers help students believe in themselves, which has a powerful impact on their lives today and in the future. This story comes from Grace, who remembers finding her own power in Mr. Fanning's classroom:

I loved school, except for physical education. I dreaded the days my class would go to PE. I was good at academics, but I felt clumsy and slow doing anything athletic. One day we had to take a physical fitness test … my nightmare. I started at the pull-up station. After trying for a few seconds, I gave up.

My teacher, Mr. Fanning, came over and knelt down next to me. He asked what thoughts were going through my head when I tried to do a pull-up. I told him that I just knew I couldn't do it, that people like me can't do things like that. He suggested that I kick that negative voice out of my head, and instead, tell myself that I am strong and capable. He said I may not get it right away, but with more empowering self-talk and practice, he just knew I could do it.

I figured I had nothing to lose, so I took Mr. Fanning's advice. I told myself that I was strong, and I practiced. It took a couple of weeks, but I finally did a pull-up. I could hear my teacher cheering from across the gym as if I had won a gold medal.

Mr. Fanning's advice has served me well, way beyond my P.E. class. I learned to catch that negative voice inside my head and stop self-doubt from creeping in. I started to talk to myself with kind and encouraging words. I began to understand that with time and practice, I could

DOI: 10.4324/9781003366423-81

do anything I set my mind to. I've carried that wisdom through every challenge since, and I'm forever grateful to Mr. Fanning.

Reflection

When they feel like they are failing, your students need coaching and practice in self-talk. These lessons can become a lasting part of your students' lives. They may need to be guided through positive thought processes and supported in the development of a new mindset. While it may not always come naturally, your students are ready to learn.

How can you help your students change limiting self-talk into empowering thoughts?

How can you incorporate mindset lessons into your content?

Who needs a little personal coaching to cultivate a positive mindset?

You make an impact when you teach them to speak to themselves positively.

Lesson 81
Being Positive

Everyone needs a kind word, a compliment, and appreciation. Even while you are building community in your classroom, you are building the esteem of individual students. This story comes from Lena, who remembers Mrs. McCall's positive reinforcement during an awkward time:

This is probably a strange thing to remember, but I have a clear memory of the mirror in my fifth-grade classroom. Between my classroom and an adjoining classroom was a restroom with a full-length mirror outside the door. Because we were getting to that self-conscious pre-teen stage, my friends and I always checked ourselves when we walked by that mirror. Instead of fussing at us to get back to our seats, Mrs. McCall found a way to leverage the power of the mirror.

Our teacher began using dry erase markers to write affirming messages on the mirror, and she changed the messages every week. I remember reading *There is no one else like you* and *You're going to do big things*. My favorite mirror message was a big arrow pointing to the center of the mirror accompanied by the words *You're one of Mrs. McCall's favorite kids*.

It was such a simple thing, but those mirror messages made a big impact. At a time in my life when I felt awkward and unsure of myself, my teacher found a way to change my self-talk. I am the parent of two pre-teens now, and I write messages on their bathroom mirror all the time. I'm grateful to Mrs. McCall for inspiring me to add a little bit of positivity to the day.

DOI: 10.4324/9781003366423-82

Reflection

Lena's story is an important reminder of the role you play in your students' lives. Even when you aren't right there, your actions and words make an impact. You have the opportunity to help students develop self-esteem, self-acceptance, and confidence.

How do you stay positive and motivated?

How are you encouraging positivity in your classroom?

Which of your students need an extra dose of positivity?

You make an impact when you inspire students to create their own optimism.

Lesson 82
Becoming More

There are times you feel called to do more – not more work, but more of what is important. It's a delight to every teacher when a student grows up and stays connected. This story comes from Leo, who remembers finding a chosen family member in his teacher, Señor Rivera:

> Our school was having a Grandparents' Breakfast to celebrate Grandparents' Day. I remember seeing the invitation and feeling so sad because my grandparents lived in Puerto Rico and couldn't attend. I'm not sure how Señor Rivera knew, but he sent a note to my mother asking if he could accompany me to the breakfast.
>
> Señor Rivera taught Spanish to our second-grade class twice a week, and everyone thought he was the coolest teacher in the school. Sometimes he brought his guitar and taught us songs in Spanish. He grew up in Puerto Rico like my parents, and I knew some of the songs. He wore silly hats and had such an engaging way of teaching us words and phrases in Spanish.
>
> Instead of feeling sad or left out, I felt proud to go to the breakfast with Señor Rivera. The other kids were envious of me as we ate and laughed and told each other stories. He told me that his grandchildren lived far away and taking me to the breakfast helped him miss them a little less. From that day on, he became a surrogate grandparent to me and continues to check on me two decades later. He's even taught my young son some songs.

DOI: 10.4324/9781003366423-83

Reflection

It is magical when the right student and the right teacher make a connection that lasts beyond their year (or years) together in the classroom. When you become a beloved mentor to a student, you have built a relationship that nurtures you both as time passes. Dancing at a wedding, meeting a newborn baby, being a listening ear, consoling a heartbreak, you are part of a precious relationship.

What do you do to nurture relationships with your students?

What is the value of students in your life?

How do you know when you have a student you will care about forever?

You make an impact when you care about students like family.

Lesson 83
Cheering Them On

What seems simple to us can be a monumental challenge to students. You may have to go out of your way for your students at times, but watching them grow is worth the extra effort. This story comes from Cora, who remembers finding support in Mrs. Norris' classroom:

> I was President of the Student Council in eighth grade, which meant that I would have to give a speech at the end of year eighth-grade assembly. I was terrified. I had no idea how to write or prepare for such a speech. Luckily, Mrs. Norris was both my English teacher and the Student Council Advisor.
>
> Every afternoon for three weeks, Mrs. Norris stayed after school to help me. She helped me edit my speech and made sure it had a clear message. Then she borrowed a podium so I could rehearse. She taught me to close my eyes and visualize giving the speech perfectly, and I did that every night before bed.
>
> On the day of the speech, Mrs. Norris gave me a pep talk and stood right offstage behind the curtain so I could see her. Whenever I felt a hint of nerves, I looked over at her smiling face. I've given countless speeches since, and I always pretend Mrs. Norris is standing offstage cheering me on.

Reflection

Mrs. Norris' commitment to her student's success is inspiring. Like her, when you go out of your way to support students and ensure their success, you are giving freely of yourself to help

DOI: 10.4324/9781003366423-84

them prepare for life. Your students are lucky to have you in their corners.

Who needs your guidance right now to move past a hurdle?

Who do you hope to inspire to the next level?

How do you reach out to a student who needs some extra confidence?

You make an impact by standing by students as they try something new.

Lesson 84
Honoring Youth

When your students are heard, they feel valued. Your invitation to express their opinions and ideas sends a powerful message. In listening, you are validating. This story comes from Easton, who remembers the lessons in and outside of Mr. Himmel's classroom:

> The thing I remember most about Mr. Himmel's 11th-grade history class was the way he made me feel important, like my ideas and opinions had value. Instead of just lecturing and presenting the facts, he always asked questions and invited us to discuss both historical and current events.
>
> Somehow, one of the kids in our class found out that Mr. Himmel read the paper every morning at the coffee shop down the street from our school. A few of us started getting up early to join him there. I didn't really like the taste of coffee (still don't), but I felt very grown-up drinking coffee and discussing the news with my teacher.
>
> I teach at a community college now, and I try to make my students feel the way I felt in Mr. Himmel's class. I want them to know that their youth does not diminish their value or the importance of their ideas. In fact, I learn as much from my discussions with them as they do from me. I live far away from where I went to high school, but I often wonder if Mr. Himmel is having coffee and reading the paper in our coffee shop.

Reflection

Many young people complain they are not heard, neither on a national or political level, nor by the adults around them. Your classroom can be an oasis where discourse is encouraged. By

DOI: 10.4324/9781003366423-85

asking for opinions and ideas about what they are learning and living, you engage your students in critical thinking. You provide a safe space for forming and sharing opinions.

What activities lend themselves most easily to discussion in your class?

What is the value of student discussion?

When do you encourage open discourse in your classroom?

You make an impact when you value and encourage your students' voices.

Lesson 85
Inspiring Perspective

When disappointment comes, your students look to you for guidance. It's important to help them see past the letdown. This story comes from Cyrus, who remembers learning about compassion and grace in Mrs. Peet's classroom:

> I grew up in a small, southern town, and high school football was everything. When I was in fourth grade, our high school team, the Bulldogs, made it to the state championship. We got out of school early to attend a parade and pep rally before the big game.
>
> I'm sorry to say the Bulldogs lost that game, and they lost by quite a lot. Heroes the day before, the team and coaches became the subjects of ruthless scrutiny. But that Monday morning, Mrs. Peet, always a source of optimism and enthusiasm, had an assignment for us. She asked us each to write a letter to the players thanking them for their hard work and for the pride they brought to our town during the season.
>
> That assignment forever changed the way I respond to games and to my favorite teams and players. I try to appreciate the excitement of the event and remember how hard the players worked to get there. I try to see the humans under the uniforms. Mrs. Peet helped me to learn that, after all, it's only a game.

Reflection

You often find a teachable moment in the midst of (classroom, school, local, national, world) turmoil. Once you have established a culture of compassion, your students look to you for guidance

DOI: 10.4324/9781003366423-86

in tumultuous times. When you capitalize on the moment, your students grow.

What are some new perspectives your students need to hear?

What do you do to help your students process disappointment or collective upset?

How can you nurture your students as they begin to see things their own ways?

You make an impact when you inspire students to see things differently.

Lesson 86
Being Yourself

You are many things to the students you see daily. To some, you're the hallway/lunch line/parking lot patrol; to others you are the font of all knowledge. Most important, of course, is that you are a real person who laughs and cries, just like them. This story comes from Gavin, who remembers realizing his teachers, Mrs. Granger and Mr. Foley, were not always such serious people:

I had two teachers in fifth grade. Mrs. Granger taught reading and writing, and Mr. Foley taught math and science. They were both tough but fair. They had high expectations and didn't put up with too much nonsense. I liked them, and I learned so much that year.

On the last day of school, our two teachers took the class to the park for a picnic. It was strange to see Mrs. Granger and Mr. Foley in shorts and T-shirts. They had several games and competitions planned for us, from relay races to tug-of-war. The day culminated with an epic water balloon fight. I loved seeing another side of my teachers. They played every game without holding back, and I had no idea Mrs. Granger was such an ace with a water balloon.

When I reflect on my years in school, the memory of that day at the park remains. I'm not sure why I remember it so clearly. I think it's because that day taught me that everyone is multi-faceted. No one is just one thing. In fact, two teachers who didn't allow much playing around could play full out when the time was right. And I will always remember them that way.

DOI: 10.4324/9781003366423-87

Reflection

Authenticity with your students is foundational to building relationships. While all adults have moments that don't need to be shared in the classroom, you can always share your personality, warmth, sense of humor, and silliness with the students who share so much of their lives with you.

Why do you still remember certain teachers from your past?

How do you share your personality in your classroom?

How can you be more authentic with your students?

You make an impact when you are authentic.

Lesson 87
Igniting Passion

It can be frustrating when students are good at something but not particularly interested. As a teacher, you never know what will spark an interest, until you strike the right match. This story comes from Harris, who remembers finding a passion for reading in Mrs. Boyd's classroom:

> I was a capable reader in fourth grade, but I wasn't motivated to read. That changed in Mrs. Boyd's class. At the end of each day, we would pack up our belongings and head over to the rug to listen to our teacher read aloud. I still remember one Friday afternoon when she was reading *James and the Giant Peach*. Mrs. Boyd stopped reading right in the middle of the most exciting part, the part where the peach started rolling down the hill. We pleaded with her to keep going, but the bell rang to dismiss us.
>
> As soon as I got into the car with my mom, I begged her to take me to the public library. I couldn't wait until Monday to find out what happened to James and his friends. I read all weekend and finished the book. I felt like I knew a big secret, but I promised my mom I wouldn't spoil it for my classmates.
>
> That began an ongoing after-school routine with my mom. We would stop at the library to get whatever book Mrs. Boyd was reading (plus a few more books). Reading became a cherished part of my bedtime routine, and it still is. I'm grateful to Mrs. Boyd for turning a passive reader into a passionate reader.

DOI: 10.4324/9781003366423-88

Reflection

When students are naturally talented at something, they may still need to find a reason to enjoy it. It can be frustrating when talented students don't engage in your lessons and activities. But finding a way to pull them in is rewarding for them (and you).

What strategies do you use to capture your students' interests?

What challenges are you facing in your classroom with bored, but talented, students?

Which students in your class could use a little academic inspiration?

You make an impact when you help students find an academic passion.

Lesson 88
Noticing Change

When you see your students each day, it is easy to note a new hairstyle or backpack, but the more subtle shifts can be harder to spot. Sometimes students try to keep the big shifts in their lives hidden, and that's when your keen observation skills matter most. This story comes from Angel, who remembers being seen in Mrs. Beam's classroom:

> I was a highly anxious overachiever in high school. I thought if I could achieve enough, my life would be perfect. Making things happen and controlling everything kept the anxious thoughts buried, but it was taking a toll on my well-being.
>
> During my junior year, Mrs. Beam (my teacher and Latin Club sponsor) noticed that I was losing weight. When we had club functions, she saw me throw away the snacks and treats that I put on my plate. I thought by not refusing them, no one would notice that I wasn't eating.
>
> My teacher kept me after a club meeting one day to tell me what she had observed. She said that she didn't have the answers, but she knew where I could get help. She said she wanted me to feel happy and free, and she knew it was possible. With Mrs. Beam's support, I got help. She gave me hope and supported me through a life-changing (and possibly lifesaving) journey.

Reflection

You are responsible for so many things each day, which is why it's remarkable how you notice even minor changes in each student's attitude, performance, mood, and even style. Often, a series of minor changes cue to you that something bigger is afoot. As a

DOI: 10.4324/9781003366423-89

caring professional, you know how to ask the right questions and how to get more support for a student in need.

When you notice a student is off, how do you address it?

When do you refer a student for help from another professional?

Who is on your radar as possibly needing intervention right now?

You make an impact when you notice student changes and offer support.

Lesson 89
Embedding Instruction

It's fair to say that sometimes we trick our students into learning. When you imbed instruction in fun, engaging, or exciting class activities, your students may not realize how much they are learning. This story comes from Amir, who remembers getting excited in Mrs. Nance's classroom:

> I remember fifth grade as the year I learned to write, thanks to Mrs. Nance. She put all the students into writing groups to work on our weekly class newspaper. Every Friday, we came up with a story idea and then worked on the story throughout the week until we submitted it the following Thursday.
>
> Our group wrote about the need for new kickballs on the playground, our favorite cafeteria selections, and the principal's new puppy. Coming up with the story content was just one part of our task. We also had to make revisions and edits to ensure our stories were well-organized, engaging, and grammatically correct.
>
> It was always exciting when Mrs. Nance put the stories together and copied the newspaper for us to take home on Fridays. The newspaper also contained important reminders and upcoming events, and because these reminders were accompanied by our stories, everyone read them. As a teacher myself now, I appreciate Mrs. Nance's brilliance. My students write a weekly newspaper, which has made them better writers and has encouraged their families to read my announcements. I hope my students remember the newspaper as fondly as I remember mine.

DOI: 10.4324/9781003366423-90

Reflection

Amir's story lifts the veil on how Mrs. Nance embedded instruction into a fun activity, giving her students choice and a chance to be creative. When your students are having fun, they work harder and feel good about the effort. There are so many ways to let students take ownership of their learning. It takes some time on the front end, but you will have a template to use and refine for years to come. More importantly, you will have students who are learning more than they realize.

What are your tricks to slide learning activities under the student radar?

What strategies do you return to year after year?

Where can you find a place for a new, creative activity in your plans?

You make an impact when you teach students while they thought they were just having fun.

Lesson 90
Giving Options

Not all teachers are ready to move to a student-led classroom. It is a big paradigm shift, and many of us feel there are things we still need to control. But, without changing everything, you can provide plenty of opportunity for student choice. This story comes from Brielle, who remembers having options in Mr. Stapes' classroom:

> I liked reading, but I hated writing book reports. I'd completed countless tedious book reports by the time I finished fifth grade. But that changed in sixth grade when I ended up in language arts class with Mr. Stapes. He was vehemently opposed to boring book reports, and we had a whole menu of options for presenting reflections on our reading.
>
> I remember kids giving speeches as their book's characters, illustrating their favorite scenes, or writing theme songs. I loved photography, and Mr. Stapes let me create a collage that represented what the main character of my book might have seen. At first it seemed like this would be easier than writing a report. It wasn't easier; I had to think deeply about the character's point of view. But the project was fun, and it allowed me to work in a way that highlighted my passions and strengths.
>
> Mr. Stapes was a model for the power of choice and creativity in learning. He realized there were many ways to assess reading comprehension, and he seemed to enjoy the presentations as much as the students. I'm a teacher now, and I love giving my students a menu of options for completing a project. I am grateful to Mr. Stapes for the inspiration.

DOI: 10.4324/9781003366423-91

Reflection

You can focus on what your students learn while providing them with options for how they learn. Leveraging your students' strengths to create a meaningful learning environment elicits more engaged students and less off-task behavior. When you allow multiple roads to the same destination, you open the door to creativity.

How do you give your students options in your curriculum?

How can you ensure all students are engaged in learning when they are working on self-led tasks?

What new options can you find to give your students choices?

You make an impact when you trust students with their own learning.

Lesson 91
Playing to Learn

Parents and early childhood educators know the value of play. Along with developing social skills, children are learning new things and expressing themselves in important ways. This story comes from Cooper, who remembers learning the value of play in Mrs. Flagg's classroom:

> Mrs. Flagg was my third-grade teacher, and she made learning fun. Every Friday, during the last part of our math lesson, we played card games. My favorite was Nifty Fifty. Each player got four cards, and those cards had to be grouped into pairs to make 2 two-digit numbers. The player whose two numbers added up nearest to 50 (without going over) won a point.
>
> We had playing-cards at my house, and I remember teaching my dad how to play Nifty Fifty. We played every evening after dinner. My dad was a quiet, stoic man, but we talked and laughed while we played the game. And as a bonus, I became super skillful at adding two-digit numbers.
>
> Looking back, I realize how much I learned in Mrs. Flagg's class. I learned academic skills and social skills when I thought I was just having fun. I've taught the card games I learned in third grade to my son, and Nifty Fifty is his favorite. It's a fun way to connect with him, and it brings back sweet memories of my favorite teacher.

Reflection

Students of all ages still want and need to play, and you can incorporate play into almost any content. A classroom full of students engaged in purposeful play sounds like a happy hum. It holds

DOI: 10.4324/9781003366423-92

a happy teacher as well, knowing you've created a fun learning environment.

How do you allow your students to engage in on-level play.

How do you engage your students in the curriculum through games?

When is the right time for your students to play to learn?

You make an impact when you create opportunities for playing to learn.

Lesson 92
Inspiring Strength

Students watch you to see who you really are and what secret talents – or powers – you have. While your talents are many and superpowers are few, you're still someone they can look up to. This story comes from Diego, who remembers looking for clues in Mr. Benson's classroom:

> Mr. Benson was my kindergarten teacher. He was tall, with dark hair and glasses, and I thought he looked just like Clark Kent (who was really Superman in disguise). I constantly looked for clues that Mr. Benson was Superman, and I found plenty of evidence.
>
> Although I never saw him fly or bend steel, Mr. Benson demonstrated bravery on multiple occasions. Once a stray dog got onto our school grounds, and he lured the dog away. A small fire started while we were in the cafeteria, and he ran back to the kitchen to help put it out. When a girl fell and got hurt on the playground, he picked her up and carried her to the office.
>
> Even though I eventually realized he was not Superman, Mr. Benson was a model of strength and character. I still try to emulate his calm, cool demeanor and willingness to help. Mr. Benson is retired now, and I recently ran into him at the grocery store. His dark hair has turned gray, and he moves a little slower, but he will always be a superhero to me.

Reflection

Though it feels as if they aren't always listening in class, your students are always watching. They notice the way you face conflict and joy, crises and quiet. They monitor the slightest changes in

DOI: 10.4324/9781003366423-93

you and assign their own meaning. When you are happy, your students feel happy; when you are strong, they are inspired to be strong as well.

How are you mindful of your disposition in the classroom?

How do you model the behaviors you would like to see from your students?

Who are your role models for strength of character?

You make an impact as a living example of strong character for your students.

Lesson 93
Building Relationships

When you do the little things to build relationships with students, they notice. It doesn't take much to create a real connection that can last a lifetime. This story comes from Libby, who remembers a relationship born in Mrs. Rafferty's classroom:

> I was so excited to start second grade and learn grown-up things, like multiplication and cursive writing. My teacher, Mrs. Rafferty, gave each student a notebook with special lined paper the day we learned our first cursive letters. She taught us a few new letters each day. We practiced forming those letters over and over, but I couldn't wait to write words and sentences.
>
> One day, Mrs. Rafferty put an envelope on my desk. Inside was a letter written just to me, but it was in cursive. It took me a few minutes, but I could read it. The letter said that my teacher was proud of my hard work, and it ended with a request to write back.
>
> Mrs. Rafferty and I wrote letters back and forth for the rest of the school year. It was a wonderful way to practice cursive, and it made me feel special. As I moved through the school years and into college, I continued to write letters to Mrs. Rafferty. She always wrote back in cursive, and she always reminded me that she was proud of me.

Reflection

Clever Mrs. Rafferty opened a dialogue to help her student practice cursive and ended up with a permanent pen pal. It is often as small and as easy as a note to begin a relationship that nurtures both teacher and student. Students feel important when

DOI: 10.4324/9781003366423-94

you connect with them. Whether it is to provide practice in the curriculum, encourage them, or praise them, you make your students feel seen when you reach out to them individually.

When do you focus on building personal relationships in the classroom?

How do you connect with students individually?

Who could use some encouragement in your classroom right now?

You make an impact when you take the time to create real connections with students.

Lesson 94
Encouraging Goals

Sometimes all it takes to inspire a student to pursue a goal is a well-placed question. When you ask students about their goals, you encourage them to dream and inspire them to act. This story comes from Amie, who remembers finding her passion in Mrs. Brach's classroom:

> When I turned 15, I started dating a football player. By the time we were seniors, he was the star quarterback. He was being recruited by several colleges, and he had so many opportunities. My life (and all my plans for the future) revolved around him. I would go wherever he went to college, and I would support him.
>
> One day, my English teacher handed back one of my essays and asked me to stay after class. Mrs. Brach told me I was a talented writer and had a promising future. She asked me what school I planned to attend and what I was interested in studying. I was a little embarrassed to admit that I had no real plans of my own.
>
> Mrs. Brach continued to encourage me. She shared information about colleges with strong writing programs, and she helped me get an essay published in a literary magazine. She kept asking if I could be anything, what would I choose. In my heart, I knew I wanted to be a journalist. It was a difficult decision, but I decided to pursue my own goals. I'm so grateful to my teacher for helping me to follow my own star, rather than ride on the coattails of a football star.

DOI: 10.4324/9781003366423-95

Reflection

There comes a time when your students will have to make plans for their futures. As a neutral adult, you have a unique place in their lives. You are someone who wants them to be happy and successful, who has no stake in their future decisions. When you encourage your students to think about their goals, you help them start planning for their own futures.

How do you integrate conversations about post-secondary life and careers into your classroom?

How can you best encourage your students to let go of others' expectations and focus on their own goals?

Why is it important to open a dialogue about the future?

You make an impact when you encourage your students' dreams, goals, and plans.

Lesson 95
Creating Fun

Creative teaching can make learning exciting, and more importantly, it can make concepts stick. When you turn a new skill or concept into a game or something fun, students remember. This story comes from Brach, who remembers enjoying learning in Miss Waverly's classroom:

> I always appreciated teachers who made learning fun, and Miss Waverly fully embodied that description. She was my sixth-grade Language Arts teacher, and she was committed to building my vocabulary. She called us Word Wizards, and since *Harry Potter* was the popular new book, we were into being wizards.
>
> Miss Waverly had a bulletin board where we could post new words we discovered. She always chose a Word of the Day, and we'd get extra credit if we could work that word into a class discussion in a meaningful way. We did crossword puzzles, played Scrabble, and created cartoons to reinforce our word lists.
>
> We had so much fun, I didn't even realize how much my vocabulary was growing. I still drop words I learned in Miss Waverly's class to impress my family and friends. I'm grateful that she found creative ways to build my skills. I remember her every time I complete a challenging crossword puzzle or dominate a lively game of Scrabble.

Reflection

Every lesson cannot be fun and games, but you find opportunities to incorporate fun. Your students deepen their understanding of concepts and also hone their social skills when lessons are

DOI: 10.4324/9781003366423-96

creative and enjoyable. Everyone wins, especially you, as your students are happily learning without realizing it.

What fun activities do you bring into your classroom?

What does student-led or active learning look like to you?

How can your students benefit from learning creatively?

You make an impact when you engage your students in learning that is fun.

Lesson 96
Sharing Time

Educators know our days don't end at the bell. More than assignments and tasks, you take home concerns about your students. When one of them needs something extra, you try to give a little more. This story comes from Darius, who remembers finding respite in time spent with Mrs. Faunce:

> When I was nine years old, I rode my bike in front of a car and was seriously injured. I had multiple surgeries and spent weeks in the hospital recovering. I felt scared and lonely, and I missed my normal routine. When I was finally allowed to have visitors, my teacher came to see me.
>
> Mrs. Faunce came into the room with a big bag full of cards and letters from my classmates. She helped me open and read each one. It was the best distraction, and it made me determined to get back to school. For the rest of my hospital stay, my teacher came to see me a couple of times a week. She always brought letters, pictures, and books. Her visits provided moments of joy during a difficult time.
>
> Looking back, I realize how busy my teacher was. She took the time to visit me and lift my spirits. It's a kindness I will never forget. I volunteer as a hospital visitor for my church now. I try to bring that same joy to those I visit as Mrs. Faunce brought to me

Reflection

One of your most precious resources is your time, and you must take care in how you spend it. But sometimes, you find a student who needs more of your time and care. When you share your

DOI: 10.4324/9781003366423-97

time with a student, as Mrs. Faunce did, you make an impact. Your efforts bring much needed comfort and joy.

What do you do when one of your students needs more of your time?

Why do you choose to spend time with students beyond your workday?

How do you know when a student needs more from you?

You make an impact when you are there when your students need you.

Lesson 97
Understanding Needs

Students don't realize how much you observe as they learn and grow in your classroom. When you notice a desire, you may find an opportunity to fulfill it. This story comes from Krystal, who remembers Mrs. Ripley's understanding and kindness:

> I was raised by a single mom who struggled to provide for me and my sister. We always had clean clothes and food to eat, but anything beyond that was a luxury. At the beginning of each school year, I envied the other kids with their new school supplies and fancy pencils. But there was one thing I coveted more than anything else … the Crayola 64-pack of crayons with the sharpener built into the box.
>
> My third-grade teacher, Mrs. Ripley, was especially kind and encouraging. Her classroom was one place I felt like I belonged, like I was just as good as everyone else. When my birthday came, my mom couldn't send in treats like other moms usually did. But to my surprise, Mrs. Ripley brought cupcakes. And when I packed to go home that day, she slipped a gift into my backpack. It was a Crayola 64-pack of crayons with the sharpener built into the box. I don't know how she knew.
>
> I think of Mrs. Ripley often. She somehow understood my needs and fulfilled them. Mostly, I remember the way she made me feel. Because of her kindness, I felt special. I felt worthy. Inspired by my favorite teacher, I try to make the people in my life feel that way, too.

DOI: 10.4324/9781003366423-98

Reflection

Each student in your classroom has unique wants and needs. Yet, you somehow find a way to notice and respond. By doing so, you send a powerful message to students. Your actions tell them they are seen and worthy.

How do you take note of a student's wants or needs?

What steps do you take to determine how you can best meet a student's need?

Who in your classroom has a special need right now?

You make an impact when you recognize and understand your students' needs.

Lesson 98
Being Human

When you are your true self, you give students permission to be themselves. They can relax and try new things. This story comes from Oscar, who remembers learning about being real from Mrs. Gaines:

My high school history teacher was (and still is) one of my all-time favorite people. When she announced that she would be hosting Crochet Tuesdays every week, I signed up to support her. She planned to teach students how to crochet, and the group would make scarves to donate to the homeless shelter.

Despite my initial hesitation, attending Crochet Tuesdays turned out to be a very wise decision. I loved listening to Mrs. Gaines tell stories and dispense advice in between crocheting lessons. And I was the only guy in the group, so I felt like I was learning all the secrets of womanhood. I fell hard for a girl sitting next to me one Tuesday afternoon, and we got married eight years later.

I gained a wife and some mad crochet skills, but there was so much more. I'll never forget going with Mrs. Gaines to deliver the scarves we'd made. The people in need were moved by the kindness, and they seemed as enamored with our teacher as we were. I realized that Mrs. Gaines was a wonderful teacher because she was a wonderful human. She was the same in and out of the classroom, and I'm grateful for the time I got to spend with her.

DOI: 10.4324/9781003366423-99

Reflection

When students have the chance to know you outside of class, they likely compare the outside you to your teacher self. You show them that even teachers are human, with interests and lives away from school. Your authenticity creates an enduring trust that results in deep learning.

How do you bring your authentic self to the classroom?

How do your students know they are seeing the real you?

What is the value of authenticity in your classroom?

You make an impact when you are true to yourself in your class-room and everywhere else.

Lesson 99
Assessing With Compassion

Traditional tests don't always accurately measure a student's learning. You have many options to determine how your students are progressing. This story comes from Marley, who remembers the weight of her test anxiety and the compassion of Mrs. McCall.

I had a failing grade in American history, even though it was my favorite class. I looked forward to it every day. My teacher, Mrs. McCall, was passionate about history and made it interesting. She made the people and places come alive. She used stories, discussions, and projects to get everyone involved. She would often assign each of us a role as a historical figure and ask us to role play an event. My grades on classwork were great; so I am sure Mrs. McCall was confused by my test scores. By the mid-point in the semester, I had failed every test.

One day, Mrs. McCall asked me to stop and see her after school. She asked me how I prepared for the tests. I told her how I used the textbook, my notes, and flashcards. I explained that I felt ready for every test, until it landed on my desk. Then I freaked out. I got anxious and couldn't remember anything. All I could focus on was the clock ticking. Mrs. McCall talked with me about the items from our last test. As we talked, I remembered the names of people, places, and even the dates. Mrs. McCall decided that I should take my tests orally with her after school.

In addition to asking me test questions orally, Mrs. McCall taught me relaxation techniques and memory tricks. My grade increased and so did my confidence. By the end of the year, I was able to pass written tests. I even got a B on my final exam. Now that I am a nursing student, I memorize so much information and frequently

DOI: 10.4324/9781003366423-100

take tests. I still use the techniques Mrs. McCall taught me. I am grateful she took the time to understand my anxiety and put such effort into helping me.

Reflection

There is sometimes an assumption that if their scores are low, students have not mastered the skills or content. Marley's memory reminds us this may not be true. Take some time today to talk to your low-performing students. Ask questions and listen. There are as many different reasons for struggling as there are struggling students. When you take the time to ask why, you can be part of a solution that will make a difference in a student's life.

Which of your students are struggling to demonstrate mastery of the content?

Which skills are causing the most struggles for your students?

What factors may be contributing to their struggles?

You make an impact when you show compassion and flexibility in the service of students' learning.

Lesson 100
Sharing Strategies

Teachers make countless decisions every day, and these include the decision to start a conversation with a student in need. This story comes from Bryan, who remembers a life-shaping conversation in Mr. Denton's classroom:

> I always struggled to make big decisions. Worrying that I'd pick the wrong option, I imagined the worst. I was sure that the option I *didn't* choose would turn out so much better than what I *did* choose. This struggle was never more evident than the decisions around applying to colleges at the end of my junior year.
>
> Luckily, I ended up in Mr. Denton's homeroom. He chatted with me about my plans, and I revealed my analysis paralysis. Then my teacher took out a piece of paper and taught me how to make a decision-tree. Each branch of the tree was an option, and each option had potential outcomes, costs, and consequences. Seeing my decision sketched out so logically on a piece of paper made it less scary and easier to make a choice.
>
> I still use Mr. Denton's decision-tree model when faced with difficult choices. He didn't need to invest so much time and energy into a homeroom student, but I'm grateful that he did. Although he didn't teach me about a particular subject, he taught me a useful life skill.

Reflection

You don't have to plan an elaborate lesson to teach something that impacts a student's life. At times, students need a friendly face, a listening ear, and some honest feedback. When you ask

DOI: 10.4324/9781003366423-101

questions, you learn about their struggles. When you understand their struggles, you can help them move forward.

When do you choose to engage with students who aren't in your class?

When is the right time to share your insight with a student?

Which students in your day would appreciate a connection with you?

You make an impact when you make connections with students who are not on your roster.

Lesson 101
Becoming a Legacy

Educators may hope to be remembered for their great lessons, but we never know what students will carry from their time in our classrooms. This story comes from Dana, who remembers how Miss Sills inspired her:

> Miss Sills was my third-grade teacher, and I wanted to be just like her. She always put her hair up in a ponytail and wore a cardigan sweater. Every day, I demanded that my mom put my hair in a ponytail, and I insisted on wearing a cardigan sweater.
>
> Even more than her appearance, I admired the way Miss Sills moved through the world. She practically glided, and she never stopped smiling. She was prone to laughing until she got the hiccups. I beamed whenever she called on me to pass out papers or help with a classroom task. I knew I wanted to be a teacher, just like Miss Sills.
>
> I stayed in contact with Miss Sills until she died in a car accident when I was in high school. It was hard to fathom how someone so full of life could be gone so quickly. I did become a teacher, just like her. And I know her legacy lives on in me. When I find myself missing her, I put on my favorite cardigan and rock a ponytail.

Reflection

Your legacy is determined by what students carry. You connect with young people as they are becoming themselves both intellectually and emotionally, and they remember this formative time. They become parents, professionals, and citizens. As such, your influence continues as ripples.

DOI: 10.4324/9781003366423-102

What do you carry with you from the classrooms in your past?

What do you hope is the legacy your students take from you?

How are you intentional about the way you move through the world?

You make an impact when your students carry a piece of your time together into their lives.

Lesson 102
Inspiring Confidence

As a teacher, you can see through the masks your students wear to what lies beneath. You know how to help students find their unique attributes and strengths. This story comes from Myah, who remembers the seeds of self-assurance found in Mr. Vincent's classroom:

> I remember walking by the art room in sixth grade and always hearing music and laughter. And so, when it came time to choose classes for seventh grade, I chose art as my elective. One of the first projects Mr. Vincent assigned was a self-portrait. Mine looked like an alien, which seemed fitting since I usually felt like an alien. I was tall and gangly, and I hadn't quite grown into my nose yet.
>
> I felt so self-conscious when Mr. Vincent mounted our portraits on tagboard and displayed them around the room. Then he gave us each a felt tip pen and asked us to write one descriptive word on the tagboard about the person in the portrait. When we finished, he sent us all back to our own self-portraits to read what others had written. I could hardly believe the complimentary words written around my portrait. People described me as unique, funny, and stylish. I took those kind words to heart, and over time, I began to see myself that way.
>
> I learned so much more than brushstrokes in Mr. Vincent's class. He taught me that we are all works of art. Our imperfections make us interesting. I'm so grateful for the perspective he gave me on art and on life.

DOI: 10.4324/9781003366423-103

Reflection

Consider Mr. Vincent's bravery when asking students to comment on each self-portrait, believing they would be kind and uplifting. Sometimes students step up because we believe they will. When you are intentional about building community, you create opportunities to build confidence.

How do you help students develop confidence?

How do you help students appreciate their unique attributes?

Who in your classroom needs some inspiration to be more self-assured today?

You make an impact when you inspire your students to have confidence in themselves.

Lesson 103
Coming Together

Just like the ingredients in a delicious dish, each of your students contributes to a vibrant community. This story comes from Everett, who remembers a powerful (and tasty) lesson in Mrs. Pembrooke's classroom:

> I have a clear memory of a class feast in November of my first-grade year. Our teacher, Mrs. Pembrooke, gave each of us a slip of paper with one ingredient to bring. I was asked to bring carrots. When I heard what my friends were bringing, I couldn't figure out what we were going to make.
>
> When I walked into the classroom on the day of the feast, Mrs. Pembrooke had a few big crock pots plugged in. She helped me cut up the carrots and divide them into the pots. She did the same thing when a friend brought celery, and another brought potatoes. Once all the ingredients were in, she added some broth to each pot. By the time the feast was ready, the room smelled so good.
>
> I was amazed at how all our ingredients made the most delicious soup. I went to a diverse school, and just like that soup, the variety made it better. I make vegetable soup at home for my kids now, and the smell always reminds me of that special day in Mrs. Pembrooke's class.

Reflection

When students take part in creating something bigger than themselves, they learn to appreciate the power of the group. They feel like part of a team. And appreciating each team member's contribution helps them learn to appreciate the beauty of diversity.

DOI: 10.4324/9781003366423-104

What opportunities do you find to let your students work together?

What problems or tasks are best approached by a team?

How do you help them learn the value of working with peers?

You make an impact when you teach your students to be part of a team.

Lesson 104
Showing Pride

As much as you want your students to succeed, they want you to be proud of their successes. You show your pride when you celebrate each step toward a goal. This story comes from Tianna, who remembers making her teacher, Mrs. Silver, proud:

> Mrs. Silver's psychology class was my favorite class in high school. I liked it so much that I chose to major in psychology when I went to college. I was excited to receive an email from Mrs. Silver at the end of the spring semester. She invited me to be a guest speaker in her class, and I immediately accepted her invitation. I was a little nervous, but mostly I was excited to see my teacher again.
>
> When I arrived at Mrs. Silver's classroom, she introduced me as the guest lecturer. While I did my presentation on contingent rewards, I noticed Mrs. Silver in the back of the room beaming with pride. It felt so good to show her what I'd learned and how I'd grown.
>
> I stayed in school, earned a graduate degree, and became a school counselor. I continued to be Mrs. Silver's guest lecturer until she retired. She helped me find my passion and my career path, and she helped me discover the joy in working with young people. I hope I continue to make her proud.

Reflection

Watching your students realize a dream is a beautiful thing, made more delightful when that dream began in your classroom. No matter how old they grow, they will always be your students. Your words of affirmation and your pride might just be their greatest reward.

DOI: 10.4324/9781003366423-105

Who was the teacher you wanted to make proud?

Who in your classroom needs you to be proud of their progress?

How do you encourage your students to stay in contact so you can continue to celebrate them?

You make an impact when you simply tell your students you are proud of them.

Lesson 105
Connecting Dots

Some students have talents they just can't keep hidden. When we help them channel those impulses, their talents grow. This story comes from Roger, who remembers developing skills in Mr. Dolans' classroom:

> I was always a busy kid, and I fidgeted with everything. I remember my teachers taking things away from me in hopes that I would be still and pay attention. Unfortunately for them, my favorite thing to do was tap on my desk and books.
>
> When I was in third grade, our school got a new music teacher. His name was Mr. Dolans, and he brought something of his own to the music room … a drum kit. I still remember him playing the drums for us. Everything changed for me in that moment. I knew I couldn't quite do it yet, but I understood it. I was a drummer.
>
> Mr. Dolans spent so much time talking to me about drumming and teaching me how to play. I feel most at home behind my drums, and it all started in that music room. I'm grateful to Mr. Dolans for helping me find my passion and for nurturing it.

Reflection

Sometimes a student realizes a special talent in the classroom. Meeting the right teacher at the right time can lead to a lifelong pursuit. No doubt, you have been that teacher. When you see the early signs and help point students in the direction of a passion, you make their lives richer.

DOI: 10.4324/9781003366423-106

Who are your diamonds in the rough right now?

Who could use some direction toward their talents they haven't even realized yet?

What do you do to connect the dots for and with your students?

You make an impact when you see your students' talents and encourage them.

Lesson 106
Being Present

Some teachers have long-standing reputations in a school or community. The great ones never rest on their laurels. This story comes from Brynn, who remembers a special year in Mrs. McCann's classroom:

> Mrs. McCann was a legend in our town. She was the first-grade teacher who taught all my friends (and their parents) how to read. By the time I entered her class, she had taught for 40 years. My year with her would be her last, as she was planning to retire.
>
> That year, we had so many visitors, even a reporter from the paper. But Mrs. McCann didn't let anyone interrupt her teaching. She promised story time and music time every day, and she always delivered. She was a master, like a real, live Mary Poppins.
>
> In the spring, the community planted a tree in her honor. Once it was in the ground, we all stood in a circle around it and sang a song for our teacher. Mrs. McCann passed away a few years ago, but her tree stands strong. Whenever I go home for a visit, I stop by the schoolyard and visit Mrs. McCann's tree. I'm grateful that I got to spend that last magical year with a legend.

Reflection

Brynn's memory of Mrs. McCann is a reminder of how we would all like to be remembered. She was a beloved teacher who stayed completely engaged with her students through her last day in the classroom. She calls on us to focus on our students no matter

DOI: 10.4324/9781003366423-107

how many accolades we collect. This legendary teacher reminds us that the students in front of us are what matters.

Who are the legendary teachers who influenced you?

How important is your reputation as a teacher?

How do you stay focused on the students in front of you?

You have an impact when you stay in the moment with your students.

Lesson 107
Seeing Wonders

When you've been teaching for a long time, things can get a little stale. It's difficult, but important, to find your sense of awe in the things your students are learning for the first time. This story comes from Nuri, who remembers Mrs. Shettle's enthusiasm:

> I remember Mrs. Shettle's second-grade classroom as a place full of wonder. She was always bringing in things she found in her yard: birds' nests, snakeskins, and rocks. In the windows, she had sweet potatoes growing roots and vines. Back by the sink, there was a terrarium with interesting ferns and moss.
>
> In the spring, our teacher brought a container covered in netting with caterpillars and milkweed inside. For weeks, we watched as the caterpillars cocooned themselves then eventually emerged as butterflies. I have a clear memory of the day we took the butterflies outside to release them.
>
> Looking back, what really amazes me is Mrs. Shettle's excitement over all those things. She was an experienced teacher, yet she always seemed to look at the world through fresh eyes. Maybe our sense of wonder rubbed off on her. Whatever the reason, I'm grateful the way Mrs. Shettle introduced me to the ordinary miracles around me.

Reflection

You may have taught your content countless times, but students are learning it for the first time. When you can see ideas and concepts through your students' eyes, your teaching stays fresh, and

DOI: 10.4324/9781003366423-108

you become inspired all over again. Your students look for your excitement to kindle theirs. So, when you reconnect with your awe, you are nurturing them and yourself at once.

What in your curriculum has become mundane to you?

What could get you excited again about the things you teach?

Where do you find your energy and excitement for the classroom?

You make an impact when you join students as they experience the wonders you are revealing to them.

Lesson 108
Teaching Resilience

Students are bound to encounter less than ideal circumstances out in the world and teaching them how to deal with obstacles and disappointment helps them become resilient problem-solvers. This story comes from Khalid, who remembers learning how to make the best of the worst in Mr. Pace's classroom:

> I joined an entrepreneurship club in high school, and Mr. Pace was the club sponsor. He'd sold his own business a few years before and decided he wanted to teach. The club allowed him to share his life experience with us, and he told the best stories about his time as an entrepreneur.
>
> One of his favorite activities was asking us to generate a list of the worst possible business ideas. Then we picked the best worst idea and designed a business plan. It was his way of showing us that problem-solving and persistence can outperform good ideas.
>
> I learned so much about courage, tenacity, and patience in Mr. Pace's entrepreneurship club. Even though I never started my own business, those lessons have served me well. And on more than one occasion, I've had to go with the best of a bunch of bad ideas. In life, like in business, the rewards are often worth the risks.

Reflection

You have seen it before: the dejection of a student when the best laid plans don't work. Your students need to see that sometimes failure is the first step to success. Your students need to hear that there are always other options, other ways, new dreams, and unexplored paths.

DOI: 10.4324/9781003366423-109

How are you intentional about modeling resiliency?

How do you explicitly teach problem-solving techniques?

What is the value of looking at multiple options?

You make an impact when you help students become more resilient.

Lesson 109
Showing Up

Often, teachers attend their students' extracurricular games and performances to show they care. But there are times when showing up is about something bigger and means something more. This story comes from Jamie, who remembers her teacher, Ms. Kessler, as her biggest fan:

> I played basketball in high school. I was a good player, and we were a good team. But the girls' teams never got the attention that the boys' teams did. I did have one loyal and enthusiastic fan though, my English teacher, Ms. Kessler.
>
> I remember looking up into the stands during one game and seeing Ms. Kessler holding a sign with my name, number, and picture. The sign said, *That's my student!* My teacher waved that sign and cheered every time I made a good play.
>
> I can't even explain how much Ms. Kessler's support meant to me. And she didn't just support me at the games, she talked about our team in class and posted our schedule on the board. Because of her encouragement, my classmates started showing up. We won the district title that year, and I definitely think the fans helped. Ms. Kessler is a big part of my memories from that winning season.

Reflection

Jamie's memory of her basketball season demonstrates the importance of showing students what's important to them is important to their teachers. When you show up in both big and small ways, you communicate that you value your students. They see you,

DOI: 10.4324/9781003366423-110

even when they say nothing. Your support makes a win even better and a loss a little easier to bear.

How do you support your students beyond the classroom?

How are you explicitly and implicitly communicating respect to your students?

Who needs you to show up right now to feel more valued?

You make an impact when you show up to support your students.

Lesson 110
Creating Community

You may have 30 or more students in your classroom, each with their own personalities, quirks, and agendas. Yet, as unlikely as it seems, you bring them together and into community with each other. This story comes from Garrett, who remembers the strength of community in Mr. Wolfe's classroom:

> Mr. Wolfe was the coolest teacher in school, and all the kids hoped to be in his class when they got to fifth grade. When I got my class assignment, I felt like I'd won the lottery. Mr. Wolfe called our class The Wolfe Pack, and we even had a class cheer: *The Wolfe Pack is on top, and we just can't be stopped.*
>
> Mr. Wolfe reminded us that we represented the pack as we traveled around the school, and he expected us to represent it well. There was a collective sense of pride, and we didn't want to disappoint our teacher. When the fifth-grade kickball tournament came, we had no doubt that we would win. I think people in the next town could probably hear our class cheer.
>
> There was a panache that came with being a member of the pack, but more importantly, there were lessons about being part of a community. Because of Mr. Wolfe's expectations, we looked out for each other. We held ourselves to high standards. I'm grateful to Mr. Wolfe for teaching me that we are stronger and better together than any of us can be alone.

DOI: 10.4324/9781003366423-111

Reflection

Teachers know building community is vital for an engaging classroom. When you motivate your students through pride in their class, you help them see the value of collective effort. When they are part of something greater than themselves, they see themselves as important members of a community.

What is the value of community in the classroom?

What do you do to be intentional about building a bonded class?

When do you begin to build a sense of unity in your classroom?

You make an impact when you help your students come together as a community.

Lesson 111
Serving Together

When you plug students into community service, they learn more about their neighborhood and the world. Serving others may offer them an opportunity to see something in the community they hadn't noticed before. This story comes from Genesis, who remembers Mrs. Barrett's significant lesson:

> I joined a service club in high school because I thought it would look good on my college applications. I never expected it to change my perspective, but thanks to my teacher and club sponsor, Mrs. Barrett, I learned to see the world differently.
>
> Around the holidays, Mrs. Barrett signed us up for shifts at the community kitchen. We would be preparing and serving meals to families in need. I was stationed in the serving line next to my teacher, and I watched the way she interacted with the families. She asked their names and listened to their stories. She offered genuine words of care and encouragement. I was in awe of her compassion.
>
> On the ride back to school, I asked Ms. Barret about her interactions with the families. She revealed that her family had benefited from community support during difficult years when she was young. She told me that people end up in need for countless reasons, and when we extend grace instead of judgment, we can provide much needed encouragement. I think about her words and her story every time I am tempted to judge someone else. She offered a lesson in compassion, and I'm forever grateful for it.

DOI: 10.4324/9781003366423-112

Reflection

Students develop compassion by seeing the needs of others and helping to meet those needs. Often, those opportunities are outside the classroom and school. Working side by side in service is powerful modeling. As students see you extend yourself, you model compassion in action.

How do you encourage your students to serve the community?

How do you offer quiet lessons on compassion?

What is the value of joining your students in community service?

You make an impact when you show students how to give to others.

Lesson 112
Speaking Through Books

Teachers who love books and love kids are wonderful match-makers. The right book can instruct, uplift, nurture, and speak to the spirit of a student who needs it. This story comes from Dezi, who remembers a life-changing recommendation in Mrs. Farsten's classroom:

> I enjoyed reading in elementary school, but I struggled to find books I liked when I transitioned to middle school. I was becoming too old for children's books but not old enough for adult novels. Back then, there weren't as many young adult choices in the library. Luckily, my language arts teacher, Mrs. Farsten, saw herself as a matchmaker, pairing students with just the right books.
>
> First, my teacher asked a series of questions. Then she asked me to wait while she ran over to her immense bookshelf and scanned until she found the one. She smiled knowingly as she handed me a copy of *Jonathan Livingston Seagull* by Richard Bach. From the very first pages, I was hooked. The book spoke to me about freedom, individuality, and the power to make your own choices.
>
> I remain an avid reader, but very few books changed my life the way Mrs. Farsten's recommendation did. It was the right book at the right time in my life, and somehow my teacher knew it. I'm not sure how she developed her skills as a matchmaker – probably through her love of books and her affinity for her students. However it happened, I'm grateful.

DOI: 10.4324/9781003366423-113

Reflection

Teachers know the value of reading skills as a way to access content, but books are also a gateway to deep thinking and contemplation. When you sense a student needs direction, a little life advice, or an escape, the right book can fill the need. And sharing your love of reading helps your students see how a book can take them places.

When do you talk about the books you are reading with your students?

When have you shared specific books with a student who you felt could grow from reading it?

How do you encourage your students to read beyond your curriculum?

You make an impact when you show students how books can speak to them.

Lesson 113
Making a Difference

Small acts of kindness can make a big difference in a student's life. When you notice and take action, no matter how small, your students feel valued. This story comes from Valeria, who remembers the care she received in Mrs. Call's classroom:

> My mom moved away when I was very young, and my dad did his best to raise me. He sent me to school dressed and fed, but there were some things he couldn't quite master. I had long, curly, often unruly hair, and my dad gave up even trying to tame it.
>
> When I was in first grade, other kids made fun of me, and I became self-conscious about my hair. My teacher, Mrs. Call, called me into the classroom before school one morning. She opened her desk drawer and pulled out a hairbrush, barrettes, and a ribbon. She carefully brushed my hair, pulled it back, and tied it up in a ribbon. I felt so pretty.
>
> It became a daily routine, and I loved spending those few minutes with Mrs. Call. I'd missed having a mom, and when my teacher fixed my hair, it helped fill that void. It was such a simple thing, but it made a big difference in my life. I felt pretty, and I felt confident. I'm the mother of a little girl now, and unfortunately, she got my crazy hair. Every morning when I fix it, I think of Mrs. Call.

Reflection

There are times your students' needs are seemingly unrelated to academics, but responding to these needs can impact all areas of their lives. You may not remember the small moments of

DOI: 10.4324/9781003366423-114

kindness and connection, but students will carry these memories. And they will carry the sense of worthiness your kindness engendered.

How do you know who needs a little something extra from you?

How do you reach out to your students?

What small gestures made a difference to you as a student?

Your small acts of kindness make a big impact on students' lives.

Lesson 114
Fostering Growth

Growing up is challenging because it requires constant learning and adjusting. Just as your students become comfortable, you ask them to stretch a little farther. This story comes from Kelsey, who remembers developing agility and confidence in Mr. France's classroom:

> I was nervous to take Trigonometry in high school because I didn't think I was a math person. On the third day of class, I inquired about a schedule change, but Mr. France convinced me to give it a couple of weeks. Then he asked me to tell him about something I was good at, and I told him I was a competitive gymnast.
>
> Every time I started to struggle in class, he reminded me that I wasn't born knowing how to do a flip, and so, it would also take me some time to learn Trig. He said it's a myth that some people are math people, and he truly believed anyone could learn his content. Mr. France was committed to helping me grow in math and mindset.
>
> I ended up with a B in Trigonometry. It was a math miracle! Now every time I'm afraid to try something, I think of Mr. Dobbs. I remind myself that it takes time and effort to develop skills. I think about my struggles that eventually became successes. I'm grateful to my teacher for helping me learn to stick with the hard stuff.

Reflection

When you help your students develop stamina and tenacity in the classroom, you set them up for future successes. When you help them develop a mindset for growth and lifelong learning,

DOI: 10.4324/9781003366423-115

they can tackle any challenge, whether inside or outside of the classroom.

How do you communicate your tenacity and commitment to students in your classroom?

How do your students respond to your persistence?

What strategies do you use to cultivate stamina in your classroom?

You make an impact when you help students develop their own commitment to growth.

Lesson 115
Coaching Choice

Students are, at times, like small boats on a rough sea, blown back and forth by the winds around them. You can help them understand the power within them to withstand the storms of life. This story comes from Ginny, who remembers learning about choices in Mr. Dobbs' classroom:

> I had so many great teachers, but Mr. Dobbs was my favorite. He was my seventh-grade science teacher, and he taught me so much more than science concepts. I remember middle school as a time of big emotions. It seemed like my mood could change in an instant. Often my mood swings were preceded by someone else's words or actions. I could get upset just from a look someone gave as they passed me in the hall.
>
> Mr. Dobbs had a way of distilling life lessons into catchy phrases. He was always reminding me that I choose my mood, and I decide my vibe. He kept telling me that other people could only get to me if I let them. It was a radical idea, that I could choose my feelings.
>
> I'm still prone to mood swings, and I still practice that lesson from Mr. Dobbs. I become aware of my thoughts and feelings and consciously choose how I want to feel. It was one of the most useful things I learned in school. It was a lasting and impactful lesson. And although other people no longer determine how I feel, Mr. Dobbs still makes me happy.

DOI: 10.4324/9781003366423-116

Reflection

Mr. Dobbs reminds us that when we teach students important life skills, those lessons are lasting and pervasive. Students don't always understand their own power. When you help them see they are in control, they begin to make conscious choices. They realize their lives don't have to be determined by outside forces.

When did you realize that you had options in every part of your life?

When do you empower your students to make their own choices in class?

How do your students grow from making their own choices?

You make an impact when you empower students to make their own choices.

Lesson 116
Exploring to Learn

Teacher preparation programs teach about kinesthetic and inquiry-based learning – two powerful ways to engage students. When used together, these strategies can lead to learning that sticks. This story comes from Ruschel, who remembers everything about Mrs. Kelso's lessons:

> Mrs. Kelso was my sixth-grade science teacher, and she made learning fun. Although we used the textbook sometimes, most of her lessons were hands-on explorations or experiments. The one I remember most was designing a roller coaster to learn about forces and motion.
>
> Mrs. Kelso put us in groups and gave each group foam pipes, blocks, tape, and marbles. We had to have at least one hill and one loop in our coaster, and the marble had to stay in motion until it reached the bottom. Then, we had to explain how friction, gravity, and other forces impacted the marble's ride.
>
> I think I could still explain the concepts I learned in Mrs. Kelso's class. Her lessons were fun, and the learning stuck. I don't remember all of my teachers and their classes, but I have detailed memories of that science class. I wish all learning could be that enjoyable.

Reflection

There must have been plenty of trial and error in Mrs. Kelso's classroom. With thoughtful structuring of environment and assignment, she helped students take charge of their learning. When you blend the autonomy of student inquiry with hands-on

DOI: 10.4324/9781003366423-117

experimentation, you encourage your students to be active learners who engage at the deepest level.

How can you best employ kinesthetic strategies in your classroom?

How do you foster an environment of exploration?

What growth do you see in your students when they are in control of their learning?

You make an impact when you create an environment where students can experiment with new concepts and ideas.

Lesson 117
Sharing Power

Sharing power with students takes courage. But when you distribute responsibilities, students feel ownership of the classroom. This story comes from Lara, who remembers becoming responsible in Mrs. Bentley's classroom:

> I loved being in Mrs. Bentley's fourth-grade class. It always felt like a peaceful and happy space. Our teacher was structured, and everything had a place. But she was never harsh or controlling. The students were responsible for most of the procedures and for keeping the classroom organized. I remember feeling very grown-up under Mrs. Bentley's care.
>
> At the start of the next school year, I had mixed emotions. I was excited about being in fifth grade, but I missed my familiar teacher and classroom. To my delight, Mrs. Bentley invited me to come and speak to her new class. She wanted some of her former students to help the new students understand how the classroom worked and train them on the procedures. Mrs. Bentley always had a way of boosting my sense of competence.
>
> I learned many things from Mrs. Bentley, but one of the most important lessons was about sharing responsibility. As a parent now, I know that putting my children in charge of their own routines and spaces is not a burden on them, it's an opportunity. It's not easy to give away some control, but it's powerful. I'm grateful to Mrs. Bentley for that lesson.

DOI: 10.4324/9781003366423-118

Reflection

Some of the responsibilities in your classroom can be delegated in a way that helps you and shows trust in your students. When you empower them, you help your students feel strong and capable. By taking responsibility for managing the classroom, your students feel ownership and pride for what you are all accomplishing together

What are the benefits of sharing responsibilities and power in the classroom?

What kind of ownership do your students feel for your classroom?

How do you assign jobs in a way that benefits you and your students?

You make an impact when you empower your students to take responsibility.

Lesson 118
Inspiring Passion

You never know when a classroom activity is going to touch a student. It is a great feeling when students take a lesson and run with it. This story comes from Lionel, who remembers being inspired in Mr. Vachel's classroom:

> In third grade, we learned about the states that comprise the United States. I liked learning fun facts about the states and sharing those facts with my family. We had a quiz every week on a region, and we had to fill in the states in that region on a map. Our final quiz was to fill in the name of every state on a blank map of the whole country.
>
> Mr. Vachel inspired my dream of visiting every state. My mom laminated the map from my final quiz and bought me some star stickers. I began putting a star on every state we visited on vacation. It was fun to visit the states I'd learned about in class.
>
> Twenty years later, I still have my map, and I still add a sticker when I visit a new state. I've visited 48 now, and I can't wait to get to the last two. I send an email to Mr. Vachel every time I add a sticker, and I send him a photo of something fun or quirky from that state. It's great to have this ongoing connection with one of my favorite teachers.

Reflection

Lionel's story is a great reminder that you never know how a lesson, classroom activity, or project is going to inspire your students. When you engage them in purposeful lessons, those

DOI: 10.4324/9781003366423-119

lessons may become a springboard into future learning. You may be providing a map to guide them toward continued growth.

What lessons inspired you as a student?

What do you do to ensure your students leave your classroom full of inspiration to learn more?

How do you know when you have planted a seed of excitement?

You make an impact when you inspire students to keep learning.

Lesson 119
Advocating for Students

Everyone needs a champion, someone who is always on their side. Your students are the same. When they need you to speak for them, you know you must step up. This story comes from Lorelei, who remembers finding an advocate in Mrs. Tate's classroom:

> I was an average student, and I tried to always follow the rules. That's why I was so surprised and upset when I had a conflict with my high school math teacher. For some reason, that teacher decided I was disrespectful and lazy. I never did figure out why.
>
> One day, after my math teacher yelled at me in front of the class, I walked into my English class crying. My English teacher, Mrs. Tate, pulled me aside to ask what was going on. In between sobs, I told her about what had happened. She reassured me that everything was going to be ok and asked if she could advocate for me with the math teacher.
>
> I don't know what Mrs. Tate said to that teacher, but his interactions with me were much different after that. She didn't reveal much about the conversation, but she kept telling me it wasn't my fault. Looking back, I know it must have been daunting for her to have a difficult conversation with a colleague, but it meant the world to me that she did. I'm so grateful that Mrs. Tate had my back.

Reflection

It can be difficult to advocate for a student because you can never be sure how it will be received. Only you can choose when it is worth the risk to step forward on behalf of your students. As a discerning professional, you know how and when to intervene.

DOI: 10.4324/9781003366423-120

How do you know when to get involved with a student's problem?

How do you feel when you advocate for your students?

Who could use your voice of support right now?

You make an impact when you speak for students when they need you.

Lesson 120
Noticing a Knack

Seemingly small tasks and responsibilities can be a big deal to students. They show your trust and belief in students' abilities. This story comes from Gracie, who remembers an important job in Mrs. Rhinehart's classroom:

> I loved books when I was a kid, and Mrs. Rhinehart (my third-grade teacher) had the biggest book collection I'd ever seen. Students were always borrowing books from her shelves, and the area became a disorganized mess. One afternoon, I asked my teacher if I could arrange the books and organize the shelves.
>
> It took me a few afternoons to get the shelves straightened out, and then, Mrs. Rhinehart asked me to be the class librarian. I was thrilled! Our teacher got paint stir sticks for kids to mark the places where they took a book. The sticks helped them put the book back in the right spot, and I checked and straightened the shelves throughout the day.
>
> Being given responsibility for the class library made me feel capable and important. It was the start of my love for organizing spaces. I'm sure it seemed like a small thing to Mrs. Rhinehart, but it was a big deal to me. I remember her and that library with such fondness and gratitude,

Reflection

Educators wonder who their students will become someday, and students are wondering the same thing about themselves. Your classroom is one of the places where their futures begin to take root. By offering low-risk opportunities, you can help them discover who they might become.

DOI: 10.4324/9781003366423-121

What are your students' responsibilities in your classroom?

What do you do to help your students realize their strengths?

How did you discover what things are most important to you?

You make an impact when you provide students with opportunities to discover what they love.

Lesson 121
Waiving Judgment

You ask students to stretch and try new things in class every day, but students are often reluctant to risk embarrassment. Luckily, you create a safe space to take learning risks. This story comes from Mickey, who remembers Monsieur Banks:

> I started taking French in my sophomore year in high school. I was unsure about my ability to learn a new language, but I'd heard that Monsieur Banks was a great teacher. On the first day of class, he told us that we would speak only French during the last month of the school year. That seemed impossible to me at the time.
>
> Somehow, our teacher helped us become proficient in short conversations very quickly. He made it fun, and it felt like a safe space to try. He corrected our pronunciation, but never in a judgmental way. He clearly loved the language, and he wanted us to love it, too.
>
> To my surprise, I did speak only French in class by the end of the year, and although I'm a little rusty now, I still speak it fairly well. I took my spouse on a trip to France recently and impressed her with my use of the language. I'm grateful to Monsieur Banks for his patience, his passion, and the gift of a second language.

Reflection

It's easy for adults to forget what it's like to be a student, but your students can remind you through their struggles. With your support and lack of judgment, they become more comfortable taking risks. All classrooms can become judgment-free zones; all schools as well, with compassion, encouragement, and intentional modeling by caring educators.

DOI: 10.4324/9781003366423-122

What is the value of a judgment-free classroom?

What causes your students to balk at taking an educational risk?

How do students learn to be compassionate and encouraging toward each other?

You make an impact when you create an environment where everyone is safe to learn.

Lesson 122
Accepting Appreciation

Educators are accustomed to being the ones giving encouragement and appreciation. Sometimes, students want to flip the script and appreciate you. This story comes from Nanette, who remembers finding a way to give to her teacher, Mrs. Trainor:

I loved my fifth-grade teacher, Mrs. Trainor, and I wanted so badly to buy her a gift at the end of the school year. But my family struggled financially, and a gift wasn't in the budget. My mom suggested I write her a letter. So, I sat down at the kitchen table and filled a page with all the things I appreciated about my teacher. I wrote about how she always let me correct my mistakes, how she wrote encouraging words on my papers, and how she made me feel capable of accomplishing hard things.

When I arrived at school on the last day, I placed my envelope on top of the gifts piled on Mrs. Trainor's desk. She quietly called each student up as she opened each gift. When she got to my letter, I felt a bit embarrassed at my meager offering. But as she read it, she started to cry. She held it close to her heart and said it meant the world to her. Then she carefully pinned it to the bulletin board behind her desk.

Seven years later, when I was graduating from high school, I went back to visit Mrs. Trainor. I was surprised to see my letter still pinned to her board. She told me she read it whenever she was having a bad day. I'd brought another letter to her that day, one that listed all the ways she had prepared me for middle school, high school, and beyond. She pinned it next to the other letter and told me it was the best present she'd ever received.

DOI: 10.4324/9781003366423-123

Reflection

When your students show appreciation, it's affirmation of your hard work and care. Some teachers keep a box of special notes and letters from students and families, and some tape sweet mementos to the wall behind their desks. However you save these mementos, be sure to take the time to remember how you have influenced your students' lives.

What are your favorite keepsakes from your years in the classroom?

What do you do to hold on to the kind words of your students and their families?

When is the last time you looked back at your mementos?

You make an impact when you inspire students to show their appreciation.

Lesson 123
Creating Bonds

Give your students a big task to accomplish together, and by the time they finish, they will know each other better. There is no time to be shy when they have a deadline. This story comes from Joleen, who remembers finding her people in Ms. Westover's classroom:

> I was a shy kid, and I usually kept to myself. But in the fall of my sophomore year, my mom convinced me to join a club. My English teacher, Ms. Westover, was the sponsor, and she always made me feel welcome. One of the first tasks we were given was to design a float for the home-coming parade.
>
> It seemed easier to talk and interact with people when we were all busy sticking pieces of tissue paper into chicken wire. A group of five of us worked together on the float for hours, and by the time we finished, we were friends. Ms. Westover named us the Five Amigos, and from that day on, she always put us together when she assigned groups for a project.
>
> Although we went our separate ways after high school, the Five Amigos kept in touch. We still have regular reunions, and we always send pictures to Ms. Westover. I'm forever grateful for her kindness, encouragement, and the way she nurtured our friendship.

Reflection

When you draw new or shy students into a productive group, you help them make authentic connections. A shared vision or goal can be the foundation of new relationships. Peer connections are

DOI: 10.4324/9781003366423-124

important for your students, and some need a little nudge to get going.

How do you decide, other than data, which students to bring together?

How do you help students create bonds in your classroom?

Which students could use your help making new connections right now?

You make an impact when you help students create bonds with each other.

Lesson 124
Getting Playful

Your students love a little levity and change of routine. After all, laughter boosts mental and physical well-being. This story comes from Toby, who remembers the silliness in Mr. Wechel's classroom:

> When I tell people some of my favorite memories from high school come from my geometry class, they look at me like I'm crazy. But Mr. Wechel made everything fun. We played games, like Quadrilateral Bingo, and he even brought his mom in to talk about how shapes fit into quilt patterns. Of course, his mom also brought funny pictures of our teacher when he was a kid.
>
> The best day in Mr. Wechel's class was Pi Day. The week before, we all signed up to bring different kinds of pie. When March 14 finally arrived, we ate pie and competed in a problem-solving competition with solutions using the constant, pi. Mr. Wechel gave out stickers with funny sayings about being irrational but well-rounded.
>
> I tend to be serious most of the time, but Mr. Wechel taught me how to be silly. I realized I learned just as much and was just as productive when having fun. I still buy a pie every March 14, and I raise a fork to Mr. Wechel.

Reflection

One of life's joys is finding laughter and silliness in unexpected places, like math class. There is much to be said for infusing your classroom with joy, not just for entertainment purposes, but to enhance the learning environment. Do something unexpected and enjoy a little playfulness with your students.

DOI: 10.4324/9781003366423-125

What memories do you have of laughing along with funny and playful teachers?

What do you do to bring joy and a little silliness into your classroom?

When did you last laugh with your students?

You make an impact when you bring joy and laughter into the classroom.

Lesson 125
Preparing for Engagement

They may not admit it, but most of your students worry about giving class presentations and performances. You allow them to feel more comfortable with clear assignment expectations, but extra comfort comes when you prepare them to be a good audience as well. This story comes from Sawyer, who remembers gaining new skills in Mrs. Teal's classroom:

> Mrs. Teal was my sixth-grade science teacher, and she had a way of sneaking life lessons into our science lessons. I remember being very nervous about presenting my project on desert landscapes to the class, worrying I would end my last slide to critiques. I should have known that Mrs. Teal already had a plan.
>
> Before we began our presentations, our teacher instructed us to take notes so that after each presentation, we could offer one compliment and ask one question. We had to pay attention to generate a compliment and a question. And receiving compliments and questions from my classmates wasn't awkward at all. It was wonderfully validating.
>
> All these years later, whenever I'm asked to give feedback to anyone, I draft compliments and questions. It validates the work and always generates more conversation. It's such a simple but powerful structure. I'm grateful to Mrs. Teal for this and so many other lasting lessons.

Reflection

By ensuring their peers are engaged during class presentations, you allow your students to focus on their work rather than worry about what everyone else is thinking. Your clear expectations for

DOI: 10.4324/9781003366423-126

audience members set everyone up for success. And these are skills students can use now and in the years to come.

How do you prepare your students to be both presenters and audience to each other?

How do your students give each other feedback?

What is the value of having your students learn from each other?

You make an impact when you prepare students to succeed today and in the future.

Lesson 126
Deconstructing Principles

Teaching is a bit like a magic show – some sleight of hand and some skillful timing. But, unlike magicians, you reveal how everything works. This story comes from Randy, who remembers learning the trick to storytelling in Mr. Napier's classroom.:

> My fourth-grade teacher, Mr. Napier was a gifted storyteller. He had a way of integrating stories into any kind of lesson. I distinctly remember him weaving a tale about pirates and gold coins into a math lesson on long division. I'm not sure what made his stories so captivating, but he had a way of drawing everyone in.
>
> That's why I was so excited when we began a storytelling unit in the spring. Mr. Napier helped us create characters and told us the main character should be one the listener would care about. Then he instructed us to create some tension in the story, some stakes for our main character. I crafted a story about a young dragon who got lost and met a boy who helped him get home.
>
> Now that I'm a father, I love telling stories to my kids. I use all Mr. Napier's pointers, and I model my delivery after his. It's become a special bedtime activity at our house, and although I will never reach the storytelling prowess of Mr. Napier, I keep my kids entertained.

Reflection

What seems mysterious at the beginning of the year may become demystified by the end. You give your students the secrets, tricks, and tools they need. Through careful scaffolding, you deconstruct complex principles and watch your students master them.

DOI: 10.4324/9781003366423-127

Which teachers deconstructed complex curriculum into easily grasped chunks for you?

Which major concepts do your students learn best when you scaffold them?

How can you demystify without losing the rigor your students expect from you?

You make an impact when you help students experience the magic of learning.

Lesson 127
Encouraging Dreams

Young people tend to live in the now, but teachers help them think about the future. And envisioning the future can influence their decisions today. This story comes from Brayden, who remembers being pushed to examine his dream in Mrs. Kaplan's classroom:

In the fall of my freshman year in high school, my English teacher assigned a paper that ended up making a big impact on my life. Mrs. Kaplan asked us to write about a day in our lives ten tears from now. That assignment forced me to think about my goals, my values, and what I really wanted. It was surprisingly difficult.

After much thought, I wrote about working for a travel magazine. I longed to travel, and I loved taking photographs. It seemed like a dream job. But Mrs. Kaplan also prompted me to think about what it would take to get there and what I would have to sacrifice.

That paper (and Mrs. Kaplan's questions) became a guide for me. I made choices based on what would lead me closer to my dream life. I began studying travel magazines, taking photography classes, and working on my writing. I did eventually end up landing my dream job, and I did have to make many sacrifices along the way. I'm grateful to Mrs. Kaplan for helping me find my direction.

Reflection

As a teacher, you have many opportunities to help students focus on the future through assignments and conversations. Peering into the future can help your students see the path to their own success. Your class may be the gateway from where they are to where they want to be.

DOI: 10.4324/9781003366423-128

How do you engage students in thinking about their goals and dreams?

How do you encourage dialogue in your classroom about the future?

What is the importance of asking your students to focus on their future lives?

You make an impact when you encourage your students' dreams

Lesson 128
Creating Joy

Your students spend so much time in your classroom each week, it begins to feel like a second home. Like your own home, it can be infused with traditions and celebrations. This story comes from Eliza, who remembers the joy in Mrs. Pender's classroom:

> I have so many memories of my kindergarten year with Mrs. Pender. It seemed like every day was an event or celebration. But some days were even more special than others. When we went on an excursion around the school trying to catch the gingerbread man or we designed a trap to catch a leprechaun, I was certain those things were real.
>
> I distinctly remember the one hundredth day of school. We dressed up like we were 100 years old. Mrs. Pender went all out, and I hardly recognized her. We had visitors who shared their collections of 100 buttons, thimbles, and matchbooks. It was an especially memorable day.
>
> Looking back, I'm so grateful that Mrs. Pender created memorable moments for us. Now that I am a parent of young children, I try to bring some Pender magic into their days. I think I get even more joy out of our celebrations than they do, and it brings back memories of my favorite teacher.

Reflection

You create memorable moments for your students, full of excitement and learning. You help them perceive school as a welcoming and joyful place. Infusing your classroom with joyful celebrations generates memories that last a lifetime.

DOI: 10.4324/9781003366423-129

What is the purpose of creating a happy atmosphere in your classroom?

What do want your students to remember about learning with you?

Where do you draw inspiration for creating joy?

You make an impact when you create memorable moments with your students.

Lesson 129
Building a Team

Building a community in your classroom is essential. It's a contributing factor in student success – and it makes everything more fun. This story comes from Lance, who remembers uniting in pursuit of a common goal in Miss Salter's classroom:

> My middle school social studies teacher, Miss Salter, was full of energy and ideas. I loved just being around her. One day in early October, she shared an idea with our class. We would secretly learn the dance from Michael Jackson's "Thriller" video and perform it as a surprise number at the pep rally. I wasn't so sure about dancing, but nobody could say no to Miss Salter.
>
> We spent the last 15 minutes of every class pulling down the blinds and learning the dance. We didn't tell anyone about our plan. On the day of the pep rally, we were seated randomly throughout the bleachers. When the music started, we got up one by one and moved like zombies onto the gym floor.
>
> I'll never forget the cheering of the crowd as we got into our line and performed the dance. It was so much fun, and everyone loved it. It also bonded us as a class, as we became known as the Thriller class. Every October, when that song is played at a Halloween party, I still find myself dancing and remembering Miss Salter.

Reflection

You'll know you've created a cohesive team when your students unite in pursuit of a goal. It takes a strong leader to bring people together to put aside their own plans and focus on a common

DOI: 10.4324/9781003366423-130

vision. With direction and purpose, you build a team of students that will make themselves and you proud.

What can your students accomplish by working as a team?

What is the value of teamwork in a classroom?

When do you feel most inspired to work as part of a team?

You make an impact when you teach your students how to work with a team.

Lesson 130
Creating Excitement

Teaching and learning can be full of surprises. When students are on the edge of their seats, you know they are hooked. This story comes from Remi, who remembers the excitement in Mrs. Kruss' classroom:

> Mrs. Kruss was my second-grade teacher, and I remember her classroom as a happy and engaging place. She often brought in surprises for us in a big, colorful gift bag. Sometimes it was a new book, a new puzzle, or new markers for the art center. We always got excited when she brought out the bag.
>
> On one particularly memorable day, she pulled a heat lamp out. She told us that we'd be hatching baby chicks from eggs. She set up a cage in the corner, and the eggs were delivered in the afternoon. We watched and waited for them to hatch. After about a week, we noticed one of the eggs beginning to crack. We watched all day until all six of the chicks were out.
>
> I have this clear memory of that day, all of us crowded around the cage, talking in excited whispers. It seemed so miraculous, that these chirping balls of fluff were once inside eggshells. The hardware store in our town sells baby chicks every spring, and I still find myself standing and watching them. I'm grateful to Mrs. Kruss for that sweet memory.

Reflection

Remi's vivid memories are an important reminder that a bit of suspense can go a long way toward student engagement. There are so many ways to build anticipation for a unit, a day, a lesson.

DOI: 10.4324/9781003366423-131

And it's fun to watch your students guess what might happen next.

How do you create a feeling of excitement with your students?

How do you stay excited about teaching?

Why is it important to share your enjoyment of teaching and learning with students?

You make an impact when you build excitement about learning in your classroom.

Lesson 131
Building Foundations

Your students have their own goals and dreams, which they may assume exclude some of your content. But you know better, and you can help them see the relevance. This story comes from Russ, who remembers Mr. Kalna's persistence:

> Mr. Kalna was my high school English teacher, and he had high expectations. I was a football player and believed playing professional football was my future. So, I had little interest in becoming a more proficient reader and writer.
>
> But Mr. Kalna was having none of my excuses. He constantly reminded me that a good education is a privilege, and I was throwing away opportunities. He got permission from my football coach to keep me after school and help me redo papers and tests. In the end, it was easier to put forth some effort than to deal with Mr. Kalna's corrections.
>
> It turned out my teacher was right. Many of my teammates struggled in college because they didn't have a solid academic foundation. I did not make it in professional football, but I became something equally amazing – a teacher and a coach. And I constantly remind my players that a good education is a privilege.

Reflection

Adults know what can happen to the best-laid plans. Students, though, have tremendous optimism that their lives will be exactly as they've planned. You hope their dreams will become reality, even as you prepare them to have options. Your effort to keep

DOI: 10.4324/9781003366423-132

them from being single-minded keeps them from closing doors they don't yet know exist, and they will appreciate you for it.

How do you help students stay focused on foundational learning?

How do you help ensure your students have options for the future?

What are the dreams of the students in your classroom?

You make an impact when you give your students the opportunity to build a foundation.

Lesson 132
Empowering Students

When teachers notice a change in a student (even a subtle one) we ask questions. When we know what's causing the change, we are better positioned to help. This story comes from Paulina, who remembers Mrs. Handler's response to her tough news:

> My mom was diagnosed with breast cancer during my sophomore year in high school. It was scary, and I felt so helpless. Mrs. Handler, my home economics teacher, noticed that I wasn't myself. She asked me what was wrong, and I told her about my mom's diagnosis and treatment. She listened, reassured me that it would be ok, and gave me a much-needed hug.
>
> The next day in class, Mrs. Handler shared an idea. We would do a bake sale to raise funds for the American Cancer Society and make a donation in honor of my mom. I knew it wouldn't make my mom better, but it might lift her spirits. And it made me feel like I was doing something to help.
>
> We baked for a few days, then set up a table in the lunchroom. We quickly sold out of every single cookie, brownie, and cupcake. I was so excited when Mrs. Handler announced the total from our sales. I went with her to the bank to deposit our cash and get the check. I will never forget her kindness. She gave me a sense of hope and purpose during a difficult time.

Reflection

Mrs. Handler is a model for responding to student needs. She gave her student a beautiful opportunity to feel in control of her situation and helped her find an outlet for her emotions. While

DOI: 10.4324/9781003366423-133

every student's situation is different, the greatest gift in turbulent times may be a sense of empowerment, a feeling of control. And you can help provide this for them.

How do you determine what each student needs from you?

How do you help students feel empowered in their daily lives?

When do you reach out to students who are showing signs of distress?

You make an impact when you help students focus on the things they can control.

Lesson 133
Speaking Encouragement

Your students come to school from many different environments, not always warm and positive. Your class may be the bright spot in their day. This story comes from Wayan, who remembers the positivity in Mr. Kerner's classroom:

> Mr. Kerner was my sixth-grade language arts teacher. I remember him as a positive and encouraging presence during my challenging middle school years. He always found something to compliment, and he was quick with a pat on the back.
>
> One of the students in our class gifted him with a stamp that had a rock graphic and the words, "You rock!" That was his favorite phrase, and he loved using that stamp on homework and other papers. He'd even stamp it on a Post-it with a little note about something he appreciated about a student.
>
> I saved a bunch of my notes from him in a box of school memorabilia, and they remind me of the importance of words of affirmation. I try to leave the same kind of encouraging notes for family, friends, and colleagues. In the realm of influencing young lives, Mr. Kerner definitely rocked.

Reflection

Every teacher has an individual style, a persona. Your students know what to expect from you, and they look forward to seeing you each day. Your encouraging words make a big difference. Remember to give yourself some encouragement, too, because you rock.

DOI: 10.4324/9781003366423-134

How do you authentically encourage your students on a regular basis?

How do you support those who need extra encouragement at times?

What do you do to fill your own bucket when you are running low on inspiration?

You make an impact when you encourage your students whether you think they need it or not.

Lesson 134
Planning Success

It's easy to get bogged down in standards, benchmarks, and curriculum when we're trying to teach students all they need to know in a short time. But teachers somehow make time for life lessons, too. This story comes from Whitley, who remembers learning to plan in Mrs. Grier's classroom:

> I was taking several advanced classes my senior year in high school, and I felt overwhelmed by the number of projects and assignments. Luckily, my literature teacher, Mrs. Grier, taught me a strategy for managing the workload. Her backward planning system saved my sanity (and my grades) that year.
>
> Our teacher started by helping us put the due dates for all assignments in our planners. Next, we estimated how long each assignment might take. Then we scheduled the days and times we would work, taking our other obligations into account. She assured us that having it all planned out would save us from late nights and rushed papers.
>
> I followed the plan Mrs. Grier helped me create, and I never felt panicked. I continued to use her system through college, and I believe it's the reason I made the Dean's List every semester. In fact, I still use the system Mrs. Grier taught me to manage projects at work. I'm grateful for the way she set me up for success.

Reflection

Helping students learn how to manage their learning can impact their lives in the classroom and beyond. Like Whitley, your students stand to gain skills that help them prepare for whatever

DOI: 10.4324/9781003366423-135

is next in their lives. When you give your students systems and strategies, you are leaving them with more than content knowledge. You are leaving them with a workable plan for success.

What do you hope students learn from you beyond the curriculum?

What strategies do you teach explicitly to help your students prepare for life?

Why is it important to recognize teachable moments?

You make an impact when you give students lifelong strategies for success.

Lesson 135
Paying Attention

Sometimes, all your students need is your attention. When you notice and help them grow past small struggles, the big things start taking care of themselves. This story comes from Saul, who remembers Mr. Reddick's coaching:

> Mr. Reddick was my physical education teacher from third through fifth grade. He would always open up the basketball court for us before school so that we could play. I really wanted to get better at making free throws, and I used that morning time to practice.
>
> Mr. Reddick must have seen me struggling because he began to give me tips for improving. He taught me to align my front foot with the center of the rim and to angle my hips and shoulders a bit. Then he showed me how to bend my shooting arm and wrist back to make a C-shape and steady the side of the basketball with my other hand. As he watched me practice, he would remind me to focus on the basket, not the ball.
>
> Over time, I became consistently good at free throws. The extra attention from Mr. Reddick built my skills and my confidence. I applied that learning to so many other goals. Even now, when I struggle to learn a new skill, I try to break it down into steps, like Mr. Reddick did for me. And I can still dominate from the free throw line.

Reflection

Coaching gives you the opportunity to share your knowledge and skills with your students beyond the walls of the classroom. You may not be in a formal coaching role, but you can still use

DOI: 10.4324/9781003366423-136

a coaching approach. When it falls within your range of talent, coaching your students offers them the attention and guidance they need.

Why is it important to notice how your students are progressing on their own, non-curricular goals?

How do you know when to step in to offer coaching?

Who in your classroom could use your attention right now?

You make an impact when you pay attention to your students' goals and encourage them along the way.

Lesson 136
Communicating Respect

Some things seem small to us, but they are a big deal to students. When you attend to the details, your students feel important. This story comes from Ximena, who remembers Mrs. Hogan's care before she ever stepped into the classroom:

> I'm named after my grandmother, Ximena. Most people aren't sure how to say my name when they see it written. Every first day of school, when teachers called the roll, I knew they would pause when they got to my name. Many of them just asked if I had a nickname. But Mrs. Hogan, my tenth-grade math teacher, was determined to get it right.
>
> My teacher must have been looking over her student list in the days before school started because she called me at home to find out how to pronounce my name correctly. I practiced with her on the phone. I remember sitting in her class on the first day, so happy knowing that she was going to breeze through my name on the list.
>
> I know it seems like a small thing, but it meant so much to me. My name is part of my identity, and Mrs. Hogan honored that. She helped me feel known and valued.

Reflection

Your students want and deserve to feel respected. They want to know their teachers care enough to see them as unique people. You show your students you value them in countless ways, big and small. Be assured, they notice and your effort matters.

DOI: 10.4324/9781003366423-137

What makes your students feel valued and respected?

What do you think communicates your care to your students?

Which students in your day are craving respect?

You make an impact when you consistently demonstrate to your students that you respect them.

Lesson 137
Reaching Out

When students miss multiple days in a row, we wonder if they are okay. By checking in, we may find a way to help get them back. This story comes from Joseph, who remembers when Mr. Claret reached out to him:

> I'd missed a few days of school, and I was surprised to get a call from my math teacher in the afternoon. Mr. Claret said he'd missed me and was checking to see if everything was alright. I was embarrassed, but I explained that I hadn't wanted to go because I was afraid kids would make fun of my hair. My mom couldn't afford to take me to get a haircut until the end of the week, and we weren't allowed to wear hats at school.
>
> I was even more surprised when Mr. Claret knocked on my door an hour later. He brought a friend who was a barber. My teacher's friend pulled out his scissors and clippers and gave me a clean fade right in my kitchen. It was one of the best haircuts I'd ever had, and it was good to talk with these two men.
>
> It still makes me smile when I think about that day. I'm so thankful for Mr. Claret's generosity. He took the time to find out what was wrong, and then he found a way to help. Every kid needs someone like that in his life.

Reflection

When students aren't meeting your expectations, sometimes it helps to investigate. Whether the issue is classroom behavior, missing homework, failing assessments, or absences, there is often a reason. When you find the root of the problem by asking

DOI: 10.4324/9781003366423-138

a few questions, you can extend grace and assistance. Your students will be grateful you did.

How do you keep track of the things that are vying for your attention throughout the day?

How do you reach out to your students when you have concerns for them?

Who in your classroom could use some grace from you?

You make an impact when you show students you care by reaching out and checking in with them.

Lesson 138
Understanding Representation

Many people don't understand the importance of representation. Students need to see people like themselves in all places, especially in their schools. This story comes from LaRon, who remembers seeing things through fresh eyes in Mr. Wagner's classroom:

> Mr. Wagner was my high school American History teacher, and I looked forward to his class every day. He always seemed excited to teach us about our country. He used different tools beyond the textbook, and I really liked the way he used movies to teach.
>
> I remember Mr. Wagner showing the movie *Glory* when we were learning about the Civil War. It was about Robert Gould Shaw, who led the Civil War's first all-Black volunteer company. He had to deal with prejudice from the Confederates and from his own Union Army, and he fought many battles outside of the battlefield.
>
> Mr. Wagner would periodically pause the movie to lead discussions about the sacrifices of the 54th, which lost nearly half its men in the battle. He talked about how their sacrifice inspired the Union to recruit thousands more Black men for combat. The film and the discussions made the history of that time come alive. It wasn't just something printed in a textbook. It really happened, and it happened to real people. People who looked like me. I'm grateful that Mr. Wagner helped me understand the complexities of history.

DOI: 10.4324/9781003366423-139

Reflection

Students feel affirmed when they see people like themselves in leadership roles. Your students need to see how they fit into the big picture of society, and it starts when they see themselves represented in school. When you are intentional about representation, you remind students that you see them and there is a place for everyone at the table.

How conscious is your school community about representation?

How can you ensure that all students are represented in your classroom?

What is the value of representation?

You make an impact when you are intentional about representation for all students.

Lesson 139
Getting Creative

There are many ways to immerse your students in the curriculum. Thought-provoking assignments and projects help students stay engaged. This story comes from Courtney, who remembers getting inspired in Mrs. Boardman's classroom:

> My fifth-grade teacher, Mrs. Boardman, was one of the most creative teachers I had. Near the end of the year (when I'm sure we were getting restless) she found a way to get us completely engrossed in learning.
>
> Our teacher announced that we were each going to start a business. We had to figure out what we were going to offer and what we would name our companies. I loved to draw, and my business became Courtney's Cartoons. I would draw cartoons for classmates, with the customer as the main character. Once we were all ready, we traded our goods and services.
>
> I remember making business cards and advertisements for my company. Mrs. Boardman came up with math, reading, and writing lessons that revolved around our businesses. It was so much fun, and it inspired me to think about possibilities. Courtney's Cartoons did not make me rich, but it did leave me with sweet memories.

Reflection

It's exciting to think your students can learn many different standards through one engaging project. Why not divide the work and double the productivity by planning a big project with a colleague? Creating engaging and dynamic activities can be satisfying for you and impactful for your students.

DOI: 10.4324/9781003366423-140

What is the value in project-based teaching?

What units of study could be combined into a larger, multifaceted activity?

Who can you work with to get creative?

You make an impact when you find creative ways to inspire your students to learn.

Lesson 140
Rewarding Effort

Your students want to do well in school, and they usually start each school year with optimism. Luckily, you've found ways to keep them motivated and acknowledge their accomplishments. This story comes from Bree, who remembers high expectations and a delightful reward in Mrs. Knoll's classroom:

> I always worked hard in school, but Mrs. Knoll (my fourth-grade teacher) made me want to work especially hard. She assigned challenging work, but she assured me I could do it. At the beginning of the year, she promised to take anyone who earned all As on every report card out for dinner at the end of the year. It wasn't easy, but I did it.
>
> My family couldn't afford to go out for dinner, and I had only been to a restaurant a few times. Four students earned the reward, and we got all dressed up to go out with our teacher. I remember feeling so fancy using the cloth napkins and shiny utensils.
>
> I still think of that dinner often. I've had many restaurant meals in my adult life, but none have topped the meal I shared with Mrs. Knoll and my classmates. And I've earned many rewards since then, but none will ever mean more to me than that dinner.

Reflection

No doubt, Mrs. Knoll reminded her students they were working toward a major goal throughout the year, especially when their energy started to wane. There are many ways to motivate students and acknowledge both effort and achievement. A little recognition can go a long way in keeping their drive alive.

DOI: 10.4324/9781003366423-141

What motivates your students?

What is the importance of rewards, incentives, and awards?

How do you incentivize your students to focus on succeeding in your class?

You make an impact when you motivate your students and reward their efforts.

Lesson 141
Building Family

Students may end up in a class by chance, but teachers can make that random group feel like a family. And family members support each other. This story comes from Pillar, who remembers the culture in Mrs. Clifton's classroom:

> I loved being in Mrs. Clifton's fifth-grade class because she made us feel like a family. She was not just focused on our academic skills; she was also concerned with our well-being and relationships. We had a class meeting every morning, in which we talked about who was struggling, who needed support, and how we could help each other.
>
> I remember a bulletin board in our classroom where we could give a note or take a note. Our teacher put a basket of post its and markers by the board, and we were invited to write a positive message to stick on the board. And if we were having a hard time, we could take a positive message from the board.
>
> There were so many small practices and daily routines that contributed to the classroom culture. Looking back, I see how much thought Mrs. Clifton put into those things. I'm so grateful to have spent a year in that loving and supportive environment.

Reflection

Your classroom is a melting pot, full of students from different family backgrounds. Your yearly challenge is to bring them into community with each other. It might seem impossible, but you find ways to unite them. When you create a nurturing learning

DOI: 10.4324/9781003366423-142

environment, it can bloom into a supportive family for your students.

How do you create a nurturing environment for your students?

How are you intentional about creating bonds between your students?

Why is it important to create community in your classroom?

You make an impact when you build a welcoming and nurturing community your students can call home.

Lesson 142
Reframing Assumptions

Whether students enter your class with advanced knowledge or judge for themselves the first time they meet you, they think they know all about you. But first impressions aren't always accurate. This story comes from Reese, who remembers learning about expectations in Mrs. Byrd's classroom:

When I started fourth grade, I would not have guessed that Mrs. Byrd would become my favorite teacher. My previous teachers had been young and bubbly, but Mrs. Byrd was older and didn't smile the way my other teachers did. I assumed she was mean, and I begged my mom to get me moved to a different class. My mom told me to give my new teacher a chance.

I quickly adjusted to Mrs. Byrd's classroom. It was calm and structured, and I don't remember any disruptive behavior. Our teacher had high expectations, and everyone tried to meet those expectations. Mrs. Byrd was invested in our success, and she took great care in giving feedback. Because she was such a skilled teacher, I felt like I couldn't fail.

I learned so much from Mrs. Byrd, but most importantly, I learned not to make assumptions about people. She was exceptionally caring, but she showed it in her own way. She wasn't a hugger, but her words of praise made me feel just as loved. Mrs. Byrd helped me understand that there are many ways to care.

DOI: 10.4324/9781003366423-143

Reflection

There are all types of teachers, from huggers to more formal handshakers. Your students may come into your classroom full of assumptions about you, the class, and the way they will learn with you. The wonder of a new year is meeting new teachers. Once you show them who you are, and how invested you are in their success, your students learn to trust you.

What is unique or unusual about your classroom?

What assumptions do your students have about you and your class?

How do you show your students you care about them?

You make an impact when you care about students in your own authentic way.

Lesson 143
Investigating Complexity

Teachers understand human nature better than most people. We have the opportunity to help students see the humanity in all of us. This story comes from Ruben, who remembers realizing the complexities of heroes in Mr. Senz's classroom:

> Mr. Senz was my American History teacher, but he taught me so much more than timelines and dates. He taught me that we tend to remember the leaders of our past as one-dimensional heroes, but these were complex people, with strengths and flaws.
>
> He assigned each student a leader, and our job was to write a portrait of that leader. We were asked to include their contributions, leadership styles, and also their faults. I was assigned Thomas Jefferson. As expected, I included facts about his contributions as a Founding Father, author of the Declaration of Independence, and the third U.S. president. But I also had to include that he was a slave owner and did not hold the fundamental belief that people of different races had equal rights.
>
> Mr. Senz helped me see that people (even celebrated heroes) are more than just one thing. You can make great contributions to your country and still cause harm. That lesson forever changed the way I view history and the way I view any person held up as a hero.

Reflection

You are an expert in understanding human nature, as you spend every school day processing your interactions with students and observing their interactions with each other. This expertise is

DOI: 10.4324/9781003366423-144

valuable in your position, but it is valuable to your students as well. Through thoughtful classroom activities, you help students understand others better.

How are you intentional about teaching students about human nature?

How do you create opportunities to investigate questions of humanity?

Why is it important to help students understand the complexities of mankind?

You make an impact when you guide students to examine the complexities of themselves and others.

Lesson 144
Planning Positivity

Positive classroom management takes planning and patience. A cooperative class makes life easier, not just for your students, but for you as well. This story comes from Gisele, who remembers the creative behavior plan in Mrs. Marks' classroom:

> The year I spent in third grade with Mrs. Marks was an adventure. Even her classroom behavior plan was unusual and fun. Each of us had our own individual treasure map, and when we were caught being helpful or being good classroom citizens, Mrs. Marks would move us closer to the X on the map. When we reached the X, we could pick something out of her treasure chest.
>
> Our teacher also kept a big glass jar on her desk. When we did something good collectively, she put a gold coin in the jar. When the jar was full, we earned a class reward. I don't remember punishment being used in the classroom, at least not very often.
>
> Looking back, I'm amazed at how well that behavior plan worked. I loved being moved along the treasure map and hearing the gold coins clink in the jar. I don't think the rewards themselves were as motivating as the process. As a class, we encouraged and supported each other to be our best. I'm grateful for the creativity and positivity Mrs. Marks brought into the classroom.

Reflection

When you are clear about your expectations and approach students positively, they are more likely to comply and cooperate. Because your students crave all manner of success, they want to

DOI: 10.4324/9781003366423-145

please and impress you through both academics and behavior. They just need to know the target, so that they can reach it.

Who are the positive people in your building and in your life outside of school?

Who are the students who shine with positivity in your classroom?

How do you plan to create a positive environment for yourself and your students?

You make an impact when you create a positive environment for your students.

Lesson 145
Encouraging Reflection

As educators, we understand the value of reflection for learning. We help students become deep thinkers by building opportunities for reflection into daily routines. This story comes from Ross, who remembers reflecting on his life in Mrs. Zorn's classroom:

> I have so many memories from Mrs. Zorn's language arts class. I was in eighth grade and struggling to understand and express my emotions. Mrs. Zorn encouraged us to reflect on our feelings and experiences through writing.
>
> Often at the start of class, our teacher would play a song and ask us to write a reaction to the song in our journals. I remember her playing "Bridge Over Troubled Water" by Simon and Garfunkel. My father had recently moved out, and I hadn't really processed my feelings about that. The song touched something in me that morning, and I couldn't stop writing.
>
> I heard that song again the other day, and I felt like I was right back in my eighth-grade language arts classroom. Mrs. Zorn provided the space and the strategies I needed at that time in my life, and I remember her fondly.

Reflection

Life moves fast, for your students as well as you, and there is peace in slowing down to ponder things. Spending time reflecting is valuable as it gives students a chance to process and make sense of their learning. When you help them carve time out of their busy lives for contemplation, you may be teaching them a skill they will use the rest of their lives.

DOI: 10.4324/9781003366423-146

How do you make time for your own reflection, both professional and personal?

How do you integrate reflection on learning into your lessons?

What is the value of helping students make time for personal reflection in the classroom?

You make an impact when you validate your students' needs to contemplate their own thoughts.

Lesson 146
Building Esteem

In your classroom, you can easily see who lacks confidence. Along with teaching students to be kind to others, you are in the position to teach your students how to be kind to themselves. This story comes from Geri, who remembers an important lesson in Mrs. Flora's classroom:

> Mrs. Flora was definitely the right teacher at the right time in my life. She was my ninth-grade math teacher, and she taught me that how I talk to myself matters. If she heard me say anything unkind to myself, she would point it out.
>
> I was not confident at all, and I constantly compared myself to others. I decided I didn't measure up. I didn't realize how often I called myself stupid or awkward. Mrs. Flora wasn't having any of that. If she heard it, she would ask if I would say those things to a friend. Then she would make me speak to myself the way I would speak to my best friend.
>
> It sounds like such a small and silly thing, but it was powerful. Because of Mrs. Flora, I started paying attention to what I said to myself, both out loud and in my head. Speaking to myself with grace and kindness helped me begin to love myself a little more. I'm grateful to Mrs. Flora for teaching me to be my own best friend.

Reflection

Each day, you help your students build academic skills, but competence and confidence go hand in hand. As you help students feel more confident, they become willing to take academic risks and participate in their own personal growth. And a student

DOI: 10.4324/9781003366423-147

with greater self-esteem is more resilient when facing change and setbacks.

How are you intentional about helping your students build their confidence?

How do you address a specific student who is struggling with self-esteem?

Where do you find resources for lessons to build self-esteem and confidence?

You make an impact when you help your students develop a strong foundation of self-esteem.

Lesson 147
Bringing Joy

One of the joys of teaching is sharing the things you love with your students. Sometimes, those things become important to your students too. This story comes from Mason, who remembers Mrs. Haynes' joy and its unexpected influence in his life:

> I'm an awkward dancer at best. It's understandable as I come from a family of awkward dancers. But my fifth-grade teacher, Mrs. Haynes, helped me understand that when it comes to dancing, how you look is less important than how you feel.
>
> Mrs. Haynes had so much energy, and she seemed to understand that kids need to move. So, whenever we got sleepy or squirmy, she stopped instruction for a dance break. Our teacher had a CD with kid versions of pop songs. She'd pick a song, and we'd dance near our desks. She danced with us, and we all looked silly. It was pure joy and a great energy release.
>
> I still remember Mrs. Haynes saying that dancing is good for your brain and your heart. I was going through a difficult time last year; my mind and heart needed some help. I decided to put on one of those old pop songs and dance. It helped more than I expected, and it brought back joyful memories of fifth grade.

Reflection

Mason's story is an important reminder that you never know how your students will use what you share with them. By sharing what brings you joy, you invite your students to find more joy in their own lives. It's wonderful that the things you love can

DOI: 10.4324/9781003366423-148

continue to bring your students joy as they go out and navigate the world

What is the value of bringing things you love into your classroom?

What do you share with your students that brings you joy?

How do you want your students to remember the year they spend with you?

You make an impact when you share things that bring you joy with your students.

Lesson 148
Warming Kindness

Teachers are often the first to notice when a student is in need. Whether you meet that need or connect a student with someone who can, your responsiveness is impactful. This story comes from Norah, who remembers the extraordinary kindness of Mrs. Rhett:

> My family moved from Florida to Wisconsin when I was in third grade. My father had been out of work for a while, and my uncle helped him find a job there. We moved in August, but by November, the weather turned chilly.
>
> Coming from Florida, I didn't have clothes suitable for Wisconsin winter weather, and my family couldn't afford new clothes. I remember being so cold. My teacher, Mrs. Rhett, must have noticed because she showed up at my door one afternoon with a coat, sweaters, and boots in my size. I was so excited to see her and to have warm clothes.
>
> It's still the sweetest surprise I've ever had. I didn't have to pretend I wasn't cold anymore, and I looked like the other kids. Mrs. Rhett's kindness made me feel loved, and she helped me feel like I belonged in my new town. I'm forever grateful for her kindness.

Reflection

Teachers are a generous lot, giving guidance, attention, much-needed advice, and at times, material things. You can also help students access the resources they need when those are beyond your reach. When you help them get their needs met, especially in times of hardship, they remember.

DOI: 10.4324/9781003366423-149

What are the ways you give to your students?

What do you do when you notice a student in need?

Who in your classroom needs to be warmed by your generosity?

You make an impact when you show your students the generosity of kindness.

Lesson 149
Encouraging Freedom

For many of your students, the joy of learning is the freedom to create. Getting creative with the concepts they learn expands theirs skills and perspectives. This story comes from Milo, who remembers finding the freedom to experiment in Mr. Holley's classroom:

> I always liked music, but I learned to love music in Mr. Holley's class. Before that, music class seemed structured and regimented, but Mr. Holley made it spontaneous and creative. He introduced me to improvisation and jazz.
>
> Improvising with fellow musicians was freeing, but it was a little intimidating at first. Mr. Holley taught me there are no wrong notes. I only needed to focus on playing the appropriate chord tone on the right beat. As I became more comfortable with the chord changes, I got more adventurous.
>
> When we really got into a groove, there was nothing better. I lost track of time and became less self-conscious. I still love to improvise, and I'm grateful to Mr. Holley for helping me find this path to freedom, flow, and self-expression. Because of his teaching, I try to bring an improvisational spirit to my work and my life.

Reflection

When you allow your students to add their own spin to what they are studying, you honor their creative spirits. It's delightful to witness students experimenting and growing in the subject you teach. Encouraging your students to express themselves within the curriculum makes learning more individualized and engaging.

DOI: 10.4324/9781003366423-150

What assignments in your classroom allow for creativity?

What is the benefit of freedom of expression and creative license in learning?

How do you encourage your students to experiment with things they are learning?

You make an impact when you find opportunities to encourage creative freedom in your classroom.

Lesson 150
Teaching Compassionately

Teachers have a way of appreciating students as they are while also helping them grow. When you give your students respect and compassion, you help them develop. This story comes from Anya, who remembers the gentle guidance in Mrs. Forrest's classroom:

> My family moved to the United States when I was very young. My parents spoke Russian, and we all learned English together. By the time I started school, I was speaking English fluently, but I struggled with some pronunciations. Other kids often made fun of the way I said water because the w sounded more like a v.
>
> My second-grade teacher, Mrs. Forrest, had a Russian grandmother, and she could speak both languages. When we talked, she would gently help me correct my pronunciation. She had a lovely way of helping me pause and understand why a word didn't sound right. I even took the tips she gave me home to help my parents.
>
> The time and attention Mrs. Forrest invested in me helped me feel more confident. She corrected me without making me feel incompetent or devaluing my first language. I'm so grateful that she cared enough to work with me.

Reflection

Compassion and care are the cornerstones of your relationships with students. Your classroom is a safe space where students can be themselves while they are growing and changing. Your feedback is a gift and gently guides them as they develop skills and proficiencies.

DOI: 10.4324/9781003366423-151

How are you intentional about creating a safe and caring environment in your classroom?

How do you show compassion to your students?

What do you want your students to remember about the community in your classroom?

You make an impact when you create a culture of compassion with your students.

Lesson 151
Learning Preferences

Your students each have their own preferred way to learn. Your core belief that everyone can learn, just not in the same way, is evidenced as you provide different kinds of tasks. This story comes from Skylar, who remembers how Mrs. Ferriss engaged her in learning:

> I always liked school, but until fifth grade, I did not enjoy math. Reading and writing allowed me to use my imagination and make choices, but math was just about solving the problems in the book. My feelings about math changed when Mrs. Ferriss introduced me to origami.
>
> Learning about shapes by folding paper was so much more satisfying than learning about them in the math book. Origami helped me understand shapes, space, and measurement. I learned that a sheet of paper can look completely different depending on where and how it gets folded. I made the most beautiful art with a single sheet of paper and a series of folds.
>
> I still love to create through origami, and every time I do, I think of Mrs. Ferriss. As a parent now, I've taught my children how to do it. With just a sheet of paper or two, we can explore shapes and engage in real problem-solving. I'm grateful for the lesson that math is in art and in the world, not just in the textbook.

Reflection

One of the greatest challenges for a teacher is finding a way to reach a student who is struggling. Through trial and error, you figure out what works. Determining how your students learn best allows you to reach everyone in the room.

DOI: 10.4324/9781003366423-152

Why is it important to understand the learning preferences of your students?

Why do some of your students struggle to get engaged in learning activities?

How do you determine the best way to engage your students?

You make an impact when you take the time to discover how to best help your students learn.

Lesson 152
Encouraging Attempts

No matter their age, your students can become resistant to trying new things. It is often up to you to nudge them toward experiences that will enrich their lives and deepen their learning. This story comes from Barrett, who remembers finding unexpected potential in Mrs. Bond's classroom:

> I'd never thought much about poetry, until I spent a year in Mrs. Bond's class. She was my tenth-grade reading teacher, and she always selected a Poem of the Week. I remember her saying it's wonderful to sit quietly with a poem, but poetry is best when read aloud. And so, she asked for a volunteer to work on each week's poem and recite it on Friday.
>
> One day, Mrs. Bond shared an opportunity to enter the Poetry Out Loud competition. She encouraged me to select a poem from the anthology to practice for the competition. Over time, I realized that not only did I enjoy poetry, but the recitations also helped me develop confidence, presence, and a more robust vocabulary.
>
> I didn't win the competition, but it was one of my most formative high school experiences. As a leader in my organization now, I often give speeches. The strategies I learned from Mrs. Bond made me a better speaker, and I try to incorporate a poem into one of my speeches every now and then.

Reflection

Teachers are encouragers, among a thousand other things. When you recognize students' potential and gently push them in new directions, they flourish. Students will never know what they can

DOI: 10.4324/9781003366423-153

do until they try. Like Barrett, your students have nothing to lose and everything to gain by trying something new; all they need is a bit of guidance and an encouraging hand.

Who has found success when you encouraged them in new directions?

Who in your classroom right now needs a motivating nudge from you?

How do you determine who will be open to trying something new?

You make an impact when you encourage your students to grow in a new direction.

Lesson 153
Providing Context

Learners need time to contextualize new learning. You help your students prepare to learn when you give them reasons to engage and help them make connections to their knowledge base. This story comes from Colson, who remembers Mrs. Snow's practice of helping her students understand why:

> I know it's typical for a teacher to open a lesson by introducing what students will learn, but my high school biology teacher, Mrs. Snow, took it a step further. In addition to telling us what we would be learning, she always included a discussion of why we were learning it.
>
> Knowing why a topic was important and where it fit into the rest of the content was so helpful to me as a learner. In some of my other classes, new information seemed to be presented randomly, with the expectation that students would just commit it to memory. But Mrs. Snow's explanations made new concepts relevant and connected.
>
> I'm an instructor at a community college now, and I model the introductions to my lessons after Mrs. Snow. I know that understanding the why helps my students to be more engaged and remember concepts better. I'm grateful for the example of effective teaching Mrs. Snow provided.

Reflection

When we are pressed for time, educators look for ways to be more efficient, something to cut. But explaining the relevance of new learning is a valuable part of instruction. Every teacher

DOI: 10.4324/9781003366423-154

who has been asked, "Why do we need to know this?" understands that learning is all about making connections. When you are intentional about connecting new concepts to those already mastered, your students become more deeply engaged in their own learning.

How do you introduce new concepts or units in your classroom?

How does backward design help you find opportunities to contextualize new learning?

When do your students have time to make connections between skills and concepts?

You make an impact when you are intentional about why your students are learning something new.

Lesson 154
Crafting Opportunities

You teach more than standards and curriculum; you help students explore ideas and feelings. You help them understand the world. This story comes from Naomi, who remembers substantial growth in Mrs. Bartley's classroom:

> I have clear memories of my seventh-grade language arts class. My teacher, Mrs. Bartley, assigned interesting books and articles for us to read and write about. One of the most memorable projects from her class was a collection of stories from our elders.
>
> For this project, we identified an older relative or neighbor to interview. We asked questions about a major event in their lives and wrote their stories. I interviewed my grandfather who was a descendent of the Lumbee, a Native American tribe of North Carolina. Before hearing and writing his story, I didn't fully understand my own family's history.
>
> Mrs. Bartley compiled all our stories into a class anthology. That collection helped me understand my classmates and my community at a deeper level. Mrs. Bartley helped me become a better reader and writer, but she taught me so much more than literacy skills.

Reflection

Lesson planning is, in its simplest form, the creation of opportunities for growth and deepening understanding. Your lessons, activities, and projects can have a lasting influence. And students feel proud when they can draw on their own lives to create meaning for a class. There are always opportunities to honor their life experiences.

DOI: 10.4324/9781003366423-155

How do you include student experiences and outside knowledge in your class activities?

How do your students combine their perceptions with your lessons?

What curricular activities do you combine with personal exploration?

You make an impact when you create opportunities for students to link their lives to what they learn.

Lesson 155
Offering Choice

Everyone thinks and learns differently. The more strategies you share with your students, the better chance they will find what works best for them. This story comes from Aubrey, who remembers finding what works in Mr. Brewster's classroom:

> Listening to a lecture and taking notes was a typical activity in high school, but it never worked that well for me as a learner. But my high school history teacher, Mr. Brewster, taught me a way to capture the points from a lecture more effectively. He introduced me to something called Sketchnotes.
>
> Sketchnotes are a combination of writing, drawings, shapes, and graphics. With Sketchnotes, I could group related ideas or use arrows to show how things are connected. I could circle or underline key ideas. Taking notes that way required me to listen and visually connect ideas. There was something about this process that improved my learning.
>
> When I moved on to college, I continued to use Sketchnotes to capture information from lectures. I believe that practice is a big reason for my academic success. I'm so grateful that Mr. Brewster embraced innovative ideas and understood that we all think and learn differently.

Reflection

As a teacher, you have a bag of tricks to use in the classroom, so you are ready when a student needs a different approach. Your students benefit from many options, helping them develop their

DOI: 10.4324/9781003366423-156

own bag of tricks. All the reading, listening, note-taking strategies you teach, along with every graphic organizer you employ, are options for your students to use when they need them.

What are the strategies and organizers your students like the most?

What is the value of intentional instruction in how to process and gather information?

When do you offer students choice in learning strategies?

You make an impact when you help students choose what fits their needs.

Lesson 156
Partnering to Learn

It has become increasingly important to teach students how to work together. How and when students partner is each teacher's prerogative, but there's no denying how fruitful it can be for processing concepts. This story comes from Amelia, who remembers learning about partnering with a peer in Mrs. Snell's classroom:

> I was a very shy kid in elementary school, and the thought of speaking in front of the class was terrifying. Some teachers would call on me to answer a question when I didn't raise my hand. I froze, like a deer in headlights. I'm sure that anxiety didn't help me learn. But my fourth-grade teacher, Mrs. Snell, had a different way of getting students to respond.
>
> Our teacher assigned each of us a discussion partner. She would pose a question, then ask us to turn and share our answers with our discussion partners. For me, it felt like a more comfortable and safe way to process information and answer questions.
>
> As I grew older, I learned to speak up in class, but I always preferred to talk with someone near me. I wished more teachers understood how difficult it is for some students to be put on the spot. I loved Mrs. Snell for reducing my anxiety and providing a safe place to learn.

Reflection

You know teaching deepens your understanding of complex or difficult concepts, and the same can be said of your students. When one walks a peer through a problem or task (or both grapple with their learning together), everyone wins. As an added

DOI: 10.4324/9781003366423-157

bonus, by learning how to process ideas and tasks collaboratively, students prepare for a future in any profession.

What types of partnering do you ask your students to do?

What value do you find in student collaboration?

How do you teach students to work together?

You make an impact when you teach your students how to be purposeful in their collaboration.

Lesson 157
Providing Outlets

Your students have minds and hearts full of stories and ideas, but they may need help to express them. When you help students learn to express themselves in writing, you give them an outlet. This story comes from Byron, who remembers finding his voice in Mrs. Beauford's classroom:

> Mrs. Beauford was my ninth-grade English teacher. I really liked her, so I signed up for her creative writing class in tenth grade. The first thing we did every morning in creative writing was freewrite in our journals. I remember just sitting there trying to think of something to write.
>
> One morning, Mrs. Beauford suggested I write about all the things that make me angry. I started writing about my dad leaving. Then I wrote about all the assumptions made about me as a young man of color. It was like the floodgates opened. Before I knew it, I filled up two pages. My teacher let me move to a table on the side of the room so I could keep going. I wrote and wrote until the bell rang at the end of the period.
>
> I'd never felt such a release. Now, whenever I'm struggling with big feelings, I write. When I'm trying to make a big decision, I write. I've filled countless journals. I am so grateful to Mrs. Beauford for helping me see how therapeutic writing can be.

Reflection

While not every class is able to offer time for freewriting like Mrs. Beauford's class, it is certain there are times students need to express the things that are causing them pain as well as joy.

DOI: 10.4324/9781003366423-158

By helping them find an appropriate outlet, you give them a life-long strategy for clearing their minds. There are many ways your students can seek this release: meditation, drawing and coloring, writing, physical exercise, dance, music, conversation. Thanks to you, they have options.

How do you know when a student's worries are interrupting learning?

How do you encourage students to clear their minds to prepare for learning?

Who in your classroom could use some outlets to express their feelings?

You make an impact when you provide the time and opportunities for students to express their feelings.

Lesson 158
Broadening Perspectives

It's human nature to find a comfort zone, a familiar group, and stay there. But teachers know even that limits students' perspectives. Naturally, you want better for your students. This story comes from Callie, who remembers her perspective shifting in Mrs. Rosen's classroom:

> Mrs. Rosen was my math teacher and yearbook sponsor. She had a way of making everyone feel valued and important. I remember her commitment to making sure every student was represented in the yearbook, not just the popular kids.
>
> She frequently sent me to places in the school I never even knew existed to take pictures and gather quotes. I went way out to the barn in the agriculture department to see the new calf. I went to a room in the basement where students were preparing for a Dungeons and Dragons tournament. Those turned out to be some of my favorite layouts in the yearbook.
>
> While working on the yearbook, I realized how much of the school I had missed by staying in my own bubble. Mrs. Rosen taught me that everyone has a story worth telling. She taught me that all stories are equally worthy of being told. I'm so grateful for the way she shaped my perspective of our school and the world.

Reflection

The world is full of those who believe everyone thinks and lives like them. You can reduce this in your classroom by helping students get to know others and broaden their views. You can give

DOI: 10.4324/9781003366423-159

students the opportunity to form their own perspectives by considering people, places, and ideas they never knew existed.

Why is it human nature to surround ourselves with people just like us?

Why is it important to help students see new perspectives?

What can you do to encourage open-mindedness in your students?

You make an impact when you help students consider perspectives unlike their own.

Lesson 159
Starting Over

Academic skills build from year to year and course to course, so when you recognize a student's learning gaps, you understand the far-reaching consequences. Though it can be difficult to find time to reteach what a student is missing, it may be integral to success in your class and beyond. This story comes from Lorenzo, who remembers getting the foundation he needed in Mr. Rubin's classroom:

> I struggled academically in high school. My family moved often when I was younger, and my math skills never quite caught up. I was failing pre-algebra and feeling pretty hopeless. That's when Mr. Rubin started Saturday Support. He would open the school on Saturday mornings for free tutoring. Often, the students who excelled in math who needed service hours for college applications would tutor other students who were struggling.
>
> Mr. Rubin worked one-on-one with me. He wasn't my math teacher, but I think he could see I needed help. He backed way up to teach me the foundational skills I needed. Then he taught me pre-algebra skills in a way I could understand.
>
> If Mr. Rubin hadn't made the extra effort to provide Saturday Support, and if he hadn't spent time with me, I wouldn't have graduated. He made me believe that I was smart enough, just missing some pieces. I'm forever grateful for his kindness.

DOI: 10.4324/9781003366423-160

Reflection

It's satisfying to help students move from where they are to where they want to go. Perhaps no one needs you more than a student with learning gaps. There are students in your class who just need to learn (or relearn) some foundational skills before they can experience success. They all deserve a second chance at learning.

How does your school staff address learning gaps?

How do you approach a student who needs one-on-one tutoring?

Who in your classroom could use a do over, in some aspect of learning?

You make an impact when you recognize a student's need for remediation and take action.

Lesson 160
Learning by Telling

Few things solidify your students' understanding like retelling what they have learned. It's an important exercise, helping students restate concepts in their own words. This story comes from Levi, who remembers learning how to process new information in Mrs. Beal's classroom:

> Mrs. Beal was my 11th-grade literature teacher. We read some challenging books in her class, but I still remember all of them. I remember thinking *A Tale of Two Cities* by Charles Dickens had nothing to do with my life, until Mrs. Beal helped me see that it was really about hope and redemption. She said there were universal truths in all the books we were reading.
>
> As we read each one, she asked us to find another student outside our class who hadn't read the book. We were to explain it in our own words in a way this student could understand. Knowing I had to accomplish this task, I read and thought more deeply about what I was reading.
>
> Because of Mrs. Beal, I realized that I don't fully understand something until I can explain it in clear and simple terms. This realization helped me get through college as an engineering student. When I learned principles and properties, I tried to explain them to my roommates. Now I lead a team of engineers, and I attribute my success to that lesson from Mrs. Beal.

Reflection

We often think of learning as listening, but telling is powerful, too. Filtering details, highlighting what is important, and providing nuance and context show deep understanding. Retelling is

DOI: 10.4324/9781003366423-161

a powerful tool for solidifying learning and understanding. It's also a fun way to engage with others in the process.

Why does retelling and narrating their learning make an impact on your students?

Why do you encourage your students to share what they are learning at home?

How do you want your students to feel about learning in your classroom?

You make an impact when you teach your students to share what they are learning.

Lesson 161
Inquiring Minds

Teachers employ student-led discussion with the understanding that inquiry-based learning is powerful. When students prepare to confer about a lesson, concept, or text, they are deeply engaged. This story comes from Charlotte, who remembers learning to question in Mrs. Edmond's classroom:

> Most teachers ask questions at the end of a lesson, but not my sixth-grade science teacher, Mrs. Edmond. She would end every lesson by inviting us to ask her questions, and she got very excited when someone asked her a particularly challenging one.
>
> I learned to write down questions throughout the lesson so that I'd be ready for her prompt at the end. At some point it occurred to me how much more carefully I listened in Mrs. Edmond's class. Processing the information in a way that helped me craft good questions required me to actively listen.
>
> Now that I am a teacher, I appreciate her brilliance. The questions students ask give so much information about their understanding. I'm certain Mrs. Edmond could assess what we had (and hadn't) learned by the questions we asked. I'm so grateful to have had such a wonderful model for my own teaching.

Reflection

Students like to keep teachers on their toes. There is no better way than to pose their own thoughtful questions about what they are learning. With explicit instruction, your students can question the curriculum and help everyone learn more. By asking their

DOI: 10.4324/9781003366423-162

own and answering each other's questions, your students take ownership of their learning.

What is the value of inquiry-based instruction?

What ownership do your students have in their own learning process?

How do you teach students to use questioning in the classroom?

You make an impact when you empower students to question what and how they are learning.

Lesson 162
Investigating Perceptions

Your students walk into school each day with their own assumptions. You provide opportunities for them to examine, question, and rethink ideas. This story comes from Sheldon, who remembers defining his values in Mr. Tackett's classroom:

> Mr. Tackett was my tenth-grade history teacher, and his class was never boring. He always assigned interesting projects and activities based on what we were studying. When we were learning about the Civil Rights Movement in the United States, he set up trials for different historical figures, such as Rosa Parks and Malcolm X.
>
> I was assigned to the defense in the Rosa Parks trial. It was painful to have to argue why this brave woman should not be prosecuted. It seemed so obvious to me. But doing so really made me think about the context and the time. It forced me to think and helped me to define my values.
>
> So many of the projects Mr. Tackett assigned forced me to consider and defend my position. I didn't just learn about history, I learned how the past impacted my life. I'm grateful to Mr. Tackett for this deep and lasting learning.

Reflection

You provide background, explain opposing sides, and encourage research so your students can form their own opinions. However you do it, helping students question their own assumptions is important. Examining their values gives students opportunities to choose their own direction. There is nowhere better to question things than the safety of your classroom.

DOI: 10.4324/9781003366423-163

What is the value of questioning understanding?

What perceptions do you challenge your students to question?

How do you encourage your students to grow through challenging their own ideas?

You make an impact when you provide your students with opportunities to consider their values and perceptions deeply.

Lesson 163
Building Confidence

When you've built a sense of community and trust in your classroom, you can accomplish anything. Your students derive confidence from this supportive culture. This story comes from Felix, who remembers becoming sure of himself in Mrs. Noel's classroom:

> I loved Mrs. Noel's sixth-grade science class. She was always enthusiastic about her content and her students. In addition to planning great lessons, she also took us on field trips. I especially remember the trip we took to a ropes course because it prompted me to face my fear.
>
> I'd always been afraid of heights, and I wasn't sure I wanted to go on the trip. But Mrs. Noel convinced me to go. She reassured me that I would be safe and, if I could get past my fear and just start, it would be worth it. She was right. The ropes course was exhilarating, and the view from the top was amazing.
>
> I'm grateful that Mrs. Noel convinced me to go, and I'm even more grateful for the lesson she taught me that day. It's ok to be afraid, but don't let the fear stop you. In the end, the reward is worth the initial discomfort.

Reflection

You frequently build students' confidence to take academic risks. When they feel successful, they know they can take chances outside of the classroom as well. Your students' self-assurance grows because they learn to trust themselves in the safety of your leadership. The classroom community you build has a vital role in your students' development.

DOI: 10.4324/9781003366423-164

How do you show students you have faith in them?

How do you help students build their own confidence?

What are the signs you notice when a student is ready for a new challenge?

You make an impact when you believe in your students and help them believe in themselves as well.

Lesson 164
Planting Seeds

You plan ways to fan the flames of students' desires to learn, grow, and achieve success. Each student has unique interests, so you never know what will light their fires. This story comes from Mack, who remembers being sparked in Mr. Saxon's class:

> I took agriculture in middle school because it sounded like fun, and I liked being outside. In the fall, we planted seeds in small containers in the greenhouse. We tended them all winter, and by the time spring arrived, they needed bigger pots. Every spring, Mr. Saxon cleared out the greenhouse for a plant sale.
>
> To prepare for the sale, we had to calculate the cost of the seeds and the materials needed to grow the plants. We also had to consider our time and labor. It was the first time I realized that agriculture is a business. In fact, it was the first time I really understood the foundations of running a business.
>
> Mr. Saxon and the plant sale ignited an entrepreneurial spirit in me. I've started a few businesses of my own, and now I consult with young business owners to help them get started. I owe it all to the knowledge I acquired in Mr. Saxon's greenhouse.

Reflection

It took months for Mr. Saxon's whole plan to unfold, and it likely inspired many students in multiple different directions. Throughout the year, your classroom becomes a place of inspiration. You never know which students will embrace an activity or project, or which projects will start a spark. When you ignite new passions, your students learn and grow.

DOI: 10.4324/9781003366423-165

What seeds do you hope will grow in your students' lives?

What do you do to encourage your students to find what inspires them?

How do you plan for the variety of students in your classroom?

You make an impact when you help students find their own interests through your curriculum.

Lesson 165
Being Genuine

Your students want to know and understand you and the things that are important to you. When you are fearlessly yourself, your students see you as a model. This story comes from Vera, who remembers learning about integrity from her teacher, Mrs. Gannett:

> Mrs. Gannett was my high school American History teacher, and I always admired her. She wasn't afraid to speak her mind. One day, she was expressing concerns over decisions being made by our county commissioners. A classmate suggested she should run for office. And so, she soon announced her candidacy.
>
> Throughout my senior year in high school, Mrs. Gannett campaigned for county commissioner. I watched her give speeches, hold fundraisers, and knock on doors. She was a stellar debater, and she dominated her opponent. I was so proud of my teacher.
>
> She didn't win the election, but she won the respect of all the young women in our school. Mrs. Gannett modeled caring about injustice and doing something about it. She modeled courage and integrity. Most of all, she taught us that the best candidate doesn't always win, but we can't win if we don't try.

Reflection

Whoever you are and whatever your priorities, your students are always watching. Your actions communicate as much as your words, maybe more. Living with integrity, following through, and being trustworthy are all traits your students can model.

DOI: 10.4324/9781003366423-166

Through your commitment, you give them a person worthy of emulation.

Why is it important to you to be genuine and authentic in the classroom?

Why do students view their teachers as role models?

What qualities of yours would you like your students to emulate?

You make an impact when you are genuine with your students and lead by example.

Lesson 166
Getting Real

Adults can find it difficult to be vulnerable in front of children, perhaps fearing to seem weak. But students need to know you are human, just like them. This story comes from Mae, who remembers a yearlong lesson on perseverance in Ms. Nichols' classroom:

> Ms. Nichols greeted me at the door of her history classroom on my first day of eleventh grade. When she walked to the front of the room after the bell rang, I noticed she walked with a limp. As she introduced herself, she leaned against the front of her desk. She told us that she was a veteran and had lost the bottom part of her left leg in an explosion in Iraq. She lifted her pant leg a bit to show us her prosthetic.
>
> Ms. Nichols told us that when she finished rehabilitation after her injury, she wanted to do something meaningful. She said she couldn't think of anything more important than teaching us. She poured so much energy into her lessons and into each of us. She was such a passionate and dedicated teacher.
>
> I was in awe of Ms. Nichols. I know there were days when the injury she sustained in Iraq caused her pain, but she gave her all to teaching us every day. Sometimes, when I was worried about something silly and superficial, I thought about Ms. Nichols. She was open about her disability, but she never saw it as a limitation. I strive to model that same vulnerability and strength for the students I teach. Ms. Nichols will always be a model of perseverance for me.

DOI: 10.4324/9781003366423-167

Reflection

You know how important it is to model kindness, courage, and perseverance. When you are open about a challenge you are facing, you show students how to navigate obstacles. It is not always comfortable, but that openness builds trust and reminds your students that life isn't always easy.

How did you develop strength from your vulnerabilities?

How can you model the perseverance your students will need throughout their lives?

Who are your role models of perseverance?

You make an impact when you are authentic and a role model of perseverance.

Lesson 167
Negating a Narrative

Some of your students live with realities you can hardly imagine. There are many things you cannot change for them, but you can control the classroom environment. This story comes from Vivianne, who remembers finding care and compassion in Mr. Tarr's classroom:

> My dad moved out and left me with my stepmom when I was sixteen. My mom left when I was little, so living with my stepmom was my only option. She said I could stay until I turned eighteen. After both parents abandoned me, I was sure there was something wrong with me, certain I had made them want to leave.
>
> My self-esteem was low, and I looked for love and attention in unhealthy ways. Luckily, I ended up in Mr. Tarr's English class my junior year. He always complimented my writing and encouraged me to think about going to college. I told him it didn't seem like a possibility with neither parent involved in my life. He constantly reminded me that my parents' choices didn't define me.
>
> Mr. Tarr continued to check on me throughout high school, and he helped me get into college. I don't know where I might have ended up without him. I'm grateful for the many ways he built my sense of confidence and self-worth. I'll never forget his kindness.

Reflection

Every student deserves a caring teacher, but some students need it more than others. Along with teaching content, you help students build strength, hope, and self-confidence. Being an

DOI: 10.4324/9781003366423-168

encouraging voice in your students' ears takes just a little time but has tremendous returns.

How do you encourage your students to be hopeful?

What do you hope to inspire your students to do after they leave your classroom?

Which students have you watched grow beyond their circumstances?

You make an impact when you help students see their stories differently.

Lesson 168
Staying Connected

One of the reasons teachers give for returning to the classroom year after year is the connections with students. Working so closely with your learners for a school year, sometimes longer, breeds a unique type of relationship. This story comes from Dean, who remembers finding a lifelong supporter in his teacher, Mrs. Nichols:

> Mrs. Nichols was my fourth-grade teacher, and undoubtedly my favorite. She was kind, and I learned so much in her class. She was a formative part of my development as a learner and a leader. When I graduated from high school and was preparing to leave for bootcamp, I stopped by her classroom to visit her.
>
> Mrs. Nichols stayed in contact with my mom and sent me letters throughout bootcamp and as I prepared to be deployed. During my tour in Iraq, I got cards and letters from my former teacher and her fourth-grade students. That mail lifted my spirits and kept me going.
>
> I feel so lucky to have had a teacher like Mrs. Nichols in my life. She made an impact on me as a fourth grader and again as a soldier. She's no longer with us, but I will never forget her.

Reflection

While you may not stay in contact with all of them, some students will remain in your life, and you will be enriched by the continuing relationship. Today, your students can reach out to you on social media and share the moments of their lives. And they can also take note of your personal milestones. A long-term

DOI: 10.4324/9781003366423-169

relationship with a former student is unlike any other relationship; it's one to be cherished.

Why is it important to bond with your students?

Why do you stay in touch with some of your students (and your own teachers) from the past?

How do you create time and space to maintain relationships with former students?

You make an impact when you stay connected to your students and continue to be a positive force in their lives.

Lesson 169
Clarifying Dreams

You never know which students you will inspire in the classroom or where that inspiration will take them. Be assured though, you are sparking imaginations and dreams. This story comes from Laila, who remembers finding what she thought was an impossible dream in Miss Cathcart's classroom:

> I loved Miss Cathcart's class because we read great stories together, and we learned how to write our own stories. In her second-grade class, she always told us about the authors who wrote the books we read. From that time on, I dreamed of being a writer, though it didn't seem like a possibility for me.
>
> I didn't know any authors, and I couldn't imagine how a person got to be one. I'll never forget the day a real author walked into our classroom. She brought her book and talked about how she wrote it and how the book was designed and printed. Suddenly, the path seemed clearer, and my dream grew stronger.
>
> I continued to work on writing stories throughout my years in school. My first children's book is scheduled to be released in a few months, and I dedicated the book to Miss Cathcart. I'm so grateful that she helped my dream become a possibility.

Reflection

Every teaching choice you make is meant to motivate your students in some way. You hope they will be inspired to engage in class, learn more, achieve more. Some of them sail beyond your

DOI: 10.4324/9781003366423-170

hopes and end up living a dream. Some discover a lifelong passion. You never know where your students may land.

What dreams and goals of yours were born in a classroom?

How do you nurture your students' dreams for the future?

Whose dreams are you encouraging right now?

You make an impact when you help your students find their dreams and clarify their goals.

Lesson 170
Empowering Learners

Any time you make space for your students' choices and voices, they feel empowered. By empowering them, you help them grow as learners and people. This story comes from Dominic, who remembers feeling important in Mrs. Hilliard's classroom:

> Mrs. Hilliard was my third-grade teacher, and she had a way of making students feel important. Whenever we were preparing to study a new topic, she put up a piece of chart paper asking what we wanted to learn about it. We filled the chart paper with questions, and she made sure to address all of them.
>
> It seemed like an uncommon practice. Other teachers typically decided what we needed to know, and they taught that. But Mrs. Hilliard was interested in what we wanted to know. It felt like we had some power over our learning.
>
> I'm a high school science teacher now, and I always share a document with my students inviting them to post their questions and wonderings about upcoming topics and concepts. I'm grateful for Mrs. Hilliard's example of how to empower students and help them feel important.

Reflection

Teachers have expectations and pose questions, but students need us to remember they have plenty of questions and expectations of their own. When your students realize they have voice in your classroom and that you are listening, they prepare to learn differently. It is empowering for students to take part in the direction of their learning, and it helps you to understand their thinking.

DOI: 10.4324/9781003366423-171

How do you involve students in the planning for your class?

How do students respond to being empowered in your classroom?

What are the benefits and challenges of giving students choice and voice in a lesson?

You make an impact when you empower students to take part in their own learning.

Lesson 171
Connecting Community

Your classroom is a place where students try new ideas and wrestle with new concepts. As they learn, they are making decisions about themselves and choices for their futures. This story comes from Devante, who remembers connecting with a career in Mrs. Vance's classroom:

> I grew up in a community without many models for choosing a career and envisioning a future. I took a business class in high school, and my teacher assigned a paper that changed my perspective. Mrs. Vance asked us to choose a potential career and research it. We had to find out about the average pay and the job responsibilities.
>
> I chose financial planner as my prospective career. I didn't know much about it, but I'd seen someone talking about it on a television commercial. Mrs. Vance arranged a meeting for me with the planner who managed the teachers' retirement plans. He gave me so much information. And we stayed in contact until I secured an internship with him when I was in college.
>
> I enjoy my work as a financial planner now, and I feel like I'm helping people. I know I wouldn't be on this path without Mrs. Vance. I'm grateful for her inspiration, encouragement, and guidance.

Reflection

In general terms, the goal of education is to support students in creating successful futures, whatever success means to them. Teachers cannot do this alone, so bringing in community partners is a powerful practice. Your willingness to help students

DOI: 10.4324/9781003366423-172

connect with businesses and leaders in your neighborhood is one more way to encourage them to identify and pursue their goals.

How do you encourage your students to think about their futures and long-range goals?

How do you leverage your community to benefit your students?

When is the best time to help students make connections with the community outside of school?

You make an impact when you guide students in making connections relevant to their future goals.

Lesson 172
Trusting Students

Few things make your students stand taller than knowing you trust and believe in them. An excellent way to demonstrate trust and belief is to share classroom responsibilities. This story comes from Bentley, who remembers learning about working together in Mrs. Pitt's classroom:

> I loved racecars when I was a kid (still do). So, when I walked into Mrs. Pitt's third-grade classroom on the first day of school, I knew it was going to be a great year. The walls and doors were decorated in a racing theme, and there was a banner with the words, "Welcome Pitt Crew."
>
> Mrs. Pitt always referred to us as her pit crew. She taught us about a pit crew's responsibility on a racing team, and she connected that with our responsibilities in the classroom. We each had specific jobs to do, and everyone was expected to keep the classroom clean and organized. In that classroom, I felt capable and important.
>
> I took my son to a race in Daytona last year, and watching the pit crew made me think of Mrs. Pitt. I have such happy memories of my year in the Pitt Crew. In addition to reading and math, I learned the importance of collective effort and collaboration.

Reflection

When you are intentional about teaching students to work collectively toward a common goal, you shape the way they see themselves. As part of something bigger than themselves, they learn to trust each other and be accountable. Most importantly, your students are learning to trust themselves because you trust them.

DOI: 10.4324/9781003366423-173

How do you show your students that you trust them?

How do your students learn to work collaboratively?

What is the value of students sharing classroom responsibilities?

You make an impact when you entrust your students with important tasks in the classroom.

Lesson 173
Shifting Paradigms

It is not up to educators to override the values a student brings into the classroom. But we do expose students to new ideas, and we invite them to rethink old beliefs. This story comes from Darius, who remembers a paradigm shift in Miss Norton's classroom:

> Miss Norton was my fourth-grade teacher, and one of the kindest people I've ever known. She worked hard at teaching us and expected us to work hard at learning. I wasn't used to people investing in me. In the neighborhood where I grew up, it was easy to feel lost and devalued.
>
> One day, Miss Norton's father came to talk to our class about his job. He was a police officer, and most of us had learned to distrust the police. But Mr. Norton seemed nice, like his daughter. He talked about the ways he had helped people and the things he liked about his job. He helped me see that good people can become cops.
>
> I continued to stay in touch with Miss Norton as I moved through school. When I decided to become a police officer, her father became a mentor for me. They both attended the ceremony when I got my pin and badge. I continue to try to make them both proud.

Reflection

Not every student in your classroom is going to experience a change of mind, but even the smallest shift in understanding can be impactful. That shift can create the crack that lets in some light. By sharing multiple points of view, you allow students to make up their own minds. You help them consider new thoughts.

DOI: 10.4324/9781003366423-174

What strategies do you use to help your students be open to new perspectives?

What major systems of belief do you see in your classroom?

Why is it important to consider multiple points of view in the classroom?

You make an impact when you allow students to challenge their own thoughts, values, and paradigms.

Lesson 174
Launching Learning

Learning can be magical, and teachers make the magic happen. You create enchanted spaces and faraway places in the classroom. This story comes from Rory, who remembers being captivated in Mrs. Cary's classroom:

> Mrs. Cary was my second-grade teacher, and she made learning fun. I especially remember a unit she planned for us at the end of the year. That summer would be the 20-year anniversary of the Apollo 11 moon landing, and our teacher went to great effort to make our classroom feel like being on the moon.
>
> Mrs. Cary hung black paper with stars on the walls and taped crater shapes on the floors. She even convinced us to move around the room like we were in the moon's gravity. We wrote stories and drew pictures of our imagined adventures. As a culminating activity, Mrs. Cary mixed up some powdery orange Tang, and we watched a video of the landing.
>
> I became a teacher, and in Mrs. Cary's honor, I created a big celebration in my classroom for the 50-year anniversary of the Apollo 11 moon landing. The kids loved it just as much as I had 30 years before. It seems the magic of the moon still captivates.

Reflection

Every lesson may not be magical, but you create small magic every day. You invite students on exciting adventures and help them explore new worlds. Your magic stems from excellent planning and skilled teaching, but your students never need to know what is behind the curtain.

DOI: 10.4324/9781003366423-175

What have been the most powerful lessons that captivate your students?

What special events do you recognize with your students to enhance their learning?

Who were the magical teachers in your life?

You make an impact when you create magic in your classroom and in your teaching.

Lesson 175
Serving While Learning

Connecting curriculum to the service of others is a powerful practice. This story comes from Thea, who remembers the way Mrs. Burney engaged her classmates in helping her recover from loss:

> When I was 16, a fire started in the basement of my home. My family got out safely, but we lost our home and everything in it. I was devastated. We stayed with friends, and the people at our church generously donated items to help us start over. I was grateful for the help, but nothing really felt like mine.
>
> I had been taking a fashion design class at my high school. When my teacher, Mrs. Burney, heard about the fire, she decided the class would start a new project. Each of the 12 students would design a piece of clothing especially for me. They interviewed me about my favorite colors and styles, and they excitedly shared their sketches with me. My classmates worked for weeks bringing their designs to life. I had fittings, and they tailored the clothes perfectly for me.
>
> When my friends in the fashion design class finished their projects, I had a wardrobe of beautiful skirts, tops, and dresses, all made with love. I thought I'd never really recover from the fire, but I finally had clothes that felt like mine again. I'm still amazed at the thoughtful way Mrs. Burney used that project to combine learning and service. She made an undeniable impact on my life at a time when I needed it most.

DOI: 10.4324/9781003366423-176

Reflection

Thea's memory reads like a lesson plan in exemplary teaching. By meeting the need of her traumatized student through engaging her class in design, she accomplished multiple goals. She taught the value of service, reinforced skills, and modeled compassion. Mrs. Burney was a master at capitalizing on a teachable moment. By seizing the opportunity for students to learn and give, you teach them deep and lasting lessons.

What are the benefits of students serving their community?

What opportunities can you create for students to simultaneously learn and serve?

How can you provide authentic opportunities for students to apply their emerging skills?

You make an impact when you inspire students to use their emerging skills in service to others.

Lesson 176
Challenging More

Students love a challenge, though they may resist difficult tasks at times. When you meet them with challenges that are achievable, you remind them of your deep respect for them as learners. This story comes from Maia, who remembers doing more than she thought she could in Mrs. Demmi's classroom:

> My favorite class in high school was also the one in which I worked the hardest. It was Mrs. Demmi's literature class my senior year. We read challenging books and essays and responded to them in both discussions and in writing.
>
> Until Mrs. Demmi's class, I wouldn't have considered myself a strong writer. Most classes required essays that were fairly straightforward with an accompanying rubric. But Mrs. Demmi's writing assignments required me to think. She rarely gave a rubric, instead asking us to decide what would thoroughly and substantially address the prompt.
>
> Whenever we turned in a paper, Mrs. Demmi always asked the same question, "Are you proud of it?" She asked it so often that I began to ask myself that question whenever I completed an assignment. It's funny how I internalized it, and I still find myself asking it. I'm grateful to Mrs. Demmi for gently pushing me beyond what I thought I could do.

Reflection

Your students want to know you believe in their ability to meet challenges, grow, and learn. They thrive on making their own academic decisions. When you push them a little beyond their

DOI: 10.4324/9781003366423-177

comfort zones, they take great pride in their accomplishments. Then your students can look back with satisfaction and see how far they've grown.

How do ensure you are challenging your students in ways they can be successful?

How do you know when your students are proud of their progress?

Who in your classroom needs some gentle pushing to move to the next level?

You make an impact when you challenge your students in ways that help them grow.

Lesson 177
Valuing Voices

It is common for students to complain that no one ever listens to them. When you open communication in a way that gives everyone a voice, you show your students the respect they desire. This story comes from Callie, who remembers feeling validated in Ms. Jantz's classroom:

> It's difficult to explain why Ms. Jantz's classroom felt so different from most of the other classrooms I found myself in from kindergarten through grade 12. Although we were only fifth graders, Ms. Jantz treated us like we were wise and capable. She listened and valued our opinions.
>
> We had class meetings at the beginning of every day. If there was an issue, we discussed it. I remember Ms. Jantz noticing scraps and trash on our classroom floor at the end of the day and asking for suggestions. After much discussion, we decided that the best solution was for each of us to clean the area around our own desks when we packed up. Our teacher could have easily just told us to do that, but she involved us in the solution.
>
> When you are young, an adult asking for and listening to your opinion feels validating. I always felt capable and important in Ms. Jantz's class. I'm grateful for the way she built my confidence and sense of self.

Reflection

Open communication in the classroom may seem like a huge undertaking, but it's worth the effort. Your students feel valued each time you ask for their opinions, feelings, and ideas. When

DOI: 10.4324/9781003366423-178

students feel heard, they know what they have to say is important to you. It is one of the reasons they leave class feeling confident, able, and smart each day.

How do you feel when you know your voice is valued?

When do you set aside time specifically to hear the things on your students' minds?

What are the questions, ideas, concerns your students are expressing right now?

You make an impact when you show your students respect through open communication.

Lesson 178
Strategizing Together

Your classroom is full of students with individual needs, and that can be overwhelming. That's when it's important to become partners at problem-solving. This story comes from Shayne, who remembers finding the perfect strategy in Mrs. Halpburn's classroom:

> School was difficult for me. I struggled to sit still, stay focused, and complete my work. My fourth-grade teacher, Mrs. Halpburn, seemed determined to find a way to help. She never lost patience, and she approached my struggles like a puzzle to solve.
>
> She started putting a timer on my desk. If I worked until the timer buzzed, I could take a break. It was easier to focus for a short time knowing that a break was coming. As the school year went on, Mrs. Halpburn gradually lengthened the amount of time. I began to focus longer and started to complete assignments regularly.
>
> I'm still a bit restless, and I still use a timer when I need to finish a task. I'm grateful that Mrs. Halpburn didn't give up on me. She helped me to see that I was capable. I just needed to find a strategy that worked for me.

Reflection

Building a partnership with a struggling student (and the student's family) is vital to finding what works. Students may feel like failures, or like they aren't smart enough, but a simple strategy can make a big difference. When you work with students to find the right strategy, you set them on a path toward success and a lifetime of learning.

DOI: 10.4324/9781003366423-179

What are your reliable strategies for students struggling with learning tasks?

What is the value of partnering with a struggling learner to try new approaches to a problem?

How do you help students feel like part of a solution to a learning struggle?

You make an impact when you create a partnership with struggling students.

Lesson 179
Noticing Needs

It's easy to see when a student is struggling, but there isn't always an easy fix. You may have a menu of academic interventions, but social and emotional struggles are complicated. This story comes from Lucia, who remembers going through a hard time in Mrs. Helms' classroom:

> I was a shy kid, but I had a close circle of friends in high school. When I was a sophomore, my best friend went through a difficult time, and she was hospitalized after trying to harm herself. I felt so powerless to help her, and I felt lonely without her.
>
> Mrs. Helms, my English teacher, noticed that I was struggling. She checked in with me every day, and she talked with me about how my friend was doing. She helped me think about what I could say or do to support my friend. Her kindness made me feel so much better.
>
> I'm so grateful that Mrs. Helms saw me struggling and took the time to check on me. In a difficult time, she helped me feel less lonely and lost. I'm a high school teacher now, and I try to notice when my students need support. I know firsthand that a little care can make a big difference.

Reflection

You work with whole students, who bring their joys and heartaches into the classroom each day. It can be hard for them to clear their minds and focus on learning when they are very concerned about something happening elsewhere. When you care about their worries, you become someone they can trust, and in the

DOI: 10.4324/9781003366423-180

often-lonely landscape of adolescence, you help them feel less alone.

How do you know when a student needs support?

How do you approach a student who is struggling with a burden from outside the classroom?

What is the value of reaching out to your students when they need encouragement?

You make an impact when you notice a student's need and reach out to them with kindness.

Lesson 180
Knowing Students

Everyone needs a place to belong and feel appreciated. Your students are no different, and as they are developing their own identities, it may be even more important to them. This story comes from Kenzie, who remembers feeling special in Mrs. Pearle's classroom:

> Mrs. Pearle was my fourth-grade teacher, and I have so many sweet memories from my year in her class. She took the time to get to know each of her students. She celebrated our strengths and provided support when we struggled.
>
> On the last day of school, Mrs. Pearle gave each of us a letter. I read mine a hundred times. In her beautiful handwriting, she detailed what she admired about me and what she had learned from being my teacher. It made me feel known and special.
>
> Mrs. Pearle's letter is in my box of most treasured possessions. When I'm feeling low, I take it out and read it again. Reading my favorite teacher's words reminds me that I am loved and worthy. That letter is still one of the most thoughtful gifts I have ever been given.

Reflection

Getting to know your students is the best part of a new school year. They are delightful in their quirks and individuality, even when they don't see themselves that way. Your students want to be seen, and they want you to know them. Knowing them as you do, you recognize how to reach them, in good times and bad. You help them feel safe, seen, and stretched.

DOI: 10.4324/9781003366423-181

How does knowing your students help you be more effective as their teacher?

How do you get to know all your students, even the quiet ones?

Who in your classroom do you want or need to know better?

You make an impact when you demonstrate to your students that you truly know and value them.

Lesson 181
Celebrating Gains

When students have gaps in learning, they feel behind and out of step with their classmates. As you approach remediation with these students, it's most important to stay positive and encouraging. This story comes from Shep, who remembers feeling successful in Mrs. Plumb's class:

> My family moved a lot during my first few years in school. I always felt like I was behind, especially in math. When I started fourth grade, the other students already knew all the multiplication and division facts. I only knew a few.
>
> My teacher, Mrs. Plumb, made me a set of flash cards. She also made a chart of all the facts to help me track the ones I mastered. Tracking my progress increased my motivation and my confidence. Instead of making me feel behind, Mrs. Plumb celebrated my success.
>
> I will always remember that fourth-grade year as the year I became a good math student. Mrs. Plumb made sure I caught up in foundational skills and basic facts while helping me learn new skills with the other students. I'm grateful for her positivity and persistence.

Reflection

You are building your students up each day to be strong scholars, ready to learn and achieve their goals. No one needs your positivity more than students facing the challenge of remediation. Together, you and your students can celebrate gains as you fill the gaps. Be sure to take the time to celebrate those wins, small and large. Your students will appreciate your positivity, and you need to encourage yourself sometimes as well.

DOI: 10.4324/9781003366423-182

Why is remediation difficult for students?

Why is it important to build the confidence of a student who is struggling academically?

How do you diagnose gaps in learning?

You make an impact when you create a positive environment to work with students on remediation.

Lesson 182
Encouraging Action

Sometimes students struggle with small things, but they have big heartbreaks, too. They may depend on you in these times for extra kindness and a little guidance. This story comes from Vince, who remembers some good advice from his teacher, Mrs. Stouffer:

> My girlfriend of three years broke up with me in October of my senior year. I was devastated, certain that I would never feel happy again. My English teacher, Mrs. Stouffer, was always there to listen and offer support. One day, she suggested that a distraction might be helpful, and I should consider trying out for the spring play.
>
> I did audition for the play, and I was chosen for a small part. Mrs. Stouffer was right; the afternoon rehearsals were a fun distraction from my sulking and moping. I made some new friends, and we shared a lot of laughs. I even met a cute girl, and I eventually got brave enough to ask her out.
>
> Throughout that painful time, Mrs. Stouffer continued to support and encourage me. She helped lift me out of despair and gave me hope that things would get better. I'm thankful for her willingness to listen and offer advice.

Reflection

Because you remember how it felt, it can be hard to see your students suffering through hard times growing up. The fact that everyone experiences heartbreak doesn't make it easier or less important. When you listen and comfort, you validate your hurting students. You show how much you care by gently offering

DOI: 10.4324/9781003366423-183

guidance to help your students get through it. They appreciate you for being dependable as they navigate these fresh and painful situations.

How do you respond when your students tell you they are hurt?

How do you approach a student who is obviously sad, but not talking about it?

When is the right time to give advice to your students?

You make an impact when you encourage your students who are hurting.

Lesson 183
Starting Small

The old saying, "Take care of the pennies and the pounds will take care of themselves," is a bit of wisdom we all need. In a culture of instant gratification, students can forget they must work their way toward major goals by accomplishing the small ones along the way. This story comes from Sophia, who remembers the expectations in Mrs. Francis' classroom:

> Mrs. Francis was my high school biology teacher, and I was fascinated by her. She was born and raised in London, and she kept a picture of Queen Elizabeth on her desk. Her accent, her posture, and everything about Mrs. Francis seemed regal.
>
> I remember her directive when I walked into her classroom each day: "Chin up and shoulders back, Sophia." Mrs. Francis was also particular about proper speech and neat handwriting. Her high expectations came across as caring. She wanted me to succeed and believed I could.
>
> In college, I majored in biology and eventually went on to medical school. I don't know that I would have had the confidence to pursue that dream without Mrs. Francis. Because she believed in me, I learned to believe in myself. Even now, when I find myself slumping, I think of her and adjust my posture.

Reflection

The expectations in your classroom provide a foundation for excellence. Because you want the best for your students in the future, you expect their best efforts today. The seemingly minor habits your students create today will propel them forward. Every big thing starts small – it is a lesson worth teaching.

DOI: 10.4324/9781003366423-184

What habits do you hope to instill in your students?

What is the value of starting small?

How do you know when you've succeeded in helping your students establish important habits?

You make an impact when you help your students build the small habits that will serve them later.

Lesson 184
Lighting a Fire

You are a guide for the next generation of educators, and they will impact the future. This is a big responsibility, but also an honor. This story comes from Claire, who remembers how Mrs. Dyson passed the torch to a new teacher:

> Mrs. Dyson was my first-grade teacher, and for as long as I can remember, I wanted to be a teacher, just like her. I loved the books she read to us and the crafts we made at the art table in her classroom. Mostly, I loved the way she laughed. She laughed with her whole body, and she always seemed so happy to be with her students.
>
> When I was in high school, I used to come back to my elementary school to help Mrs. Dyson. She let me decorate her bulletin boards and change the books on the classroom library shelf. She always reassured me that I would be a great teacher and would make a difference.
>
> When I graduated from college and began interviewing for my first teaching job, I learned that Mrs. Dyson was retiring. I was honored (and so excited) to be hired for the first-grade position she was leaving. She left books, resources, and materials for me to use. Throughout my first year of teaching, I would find encouraging notes Mrs. Dyson had written to me tucked in spaces around the classroom. She remains my model for teaching with joy and love.

Reflection

When a teacher loves teaching, students love learning. After all, few things are more magnetic than a happy and engaged teacher. Some of your students are inspired to pursue careers as teachers

DOI: 10.4324/9781003366423-185

based on their experience with you. You never know which ones may catch the itch to teach.

How are you showing your passion for teaching when you are in the classroom?

How do you encourage students to follow their dreams for the future?

When you learn that a student wants to become a teacher, what do you say?

You make an impact when you inspire your students' passions.

Lesson 185
Celebrating Goodbye

Some students are apprehensive about summer, knowing their time in your classroom is ending. They may be nervous about what's next after they've been so happy and comfortable with you. This story comes from Savannah, who remembers a lovely goodbye in Mr. Edward's classroom:

> I loved every minute I spent in Mr. Edward's class. I was not looking forward to the last day of school because I didn't want to leave him and move on to middle school. I was so surprised when I walked up to his classroom on that last day.
>
> There was a red carpet leading up to the door, and Mr. Edward was wearing a tuxedo. There was a large sign welcoming us to The Eddies, Mr. Edward's special awards show. I'm not sure where he got a microphone, but he made a big speech before every award. We all received an Eddie, and our teacher explained why each student was deserving before presenting each award.
>
> My Eddie is still prominently displayed on my shelf. It remains my favorite of all my awards and accolades. And that day in Mr. Edward's class remains a favorite memory. What began as a sad day for me, a day of goodbyes, became a day of celebration. Mr. Edward taught me that transitions are a part of life, and a chance to reflect on what we have learned and achieved.

Reflection

The end of a school year is an exciting time, but goodbyes can be tough, especially when we are leaving a place we love. Savannah's story gives us a peek at students' feelings during those winding

DOI: 10.4324/9781003366423-186

down days. You have created many happy memories for your students. They will need some closure as you prepare to close the year, a natural transition to what comes next. Mr. Edward was as thoughtful about the year's ending as he was about the beginning.

How do you mark the end of the year and bring closure to your class?

How do you know when a student is feeling anxious about the end of the school year?

What end-of-the-year activity would nurture your spirit?

You make an impact when you acknowledge and celebrate what you have built with your students.

Final Thoughts

You did it! You've read and reflected, and you're ready to make an even bigger and more consistent impact. Never underestimate the power you have to shape students' lives, now and into the future. Remember, the lessons you teach can last for years (maybe even decades). Small moments in your classroom can stick in your students' memories for a lifetime. During this challenging time in education, we hope the stories and reflections helped you recapture the joy and find more satisfaction in teaching.

If you want to dig deeper into the origin of the stories and the research on teacher impact, check out Julie's other books:

Safe, Seen, and Stretched in the Classroom: The Remarkable Ways Teachers Shape Students' Lives

Pause, Ponder, and Persist in the Classroom: How Teachers Turn Challenges into Opportunities for Impact

And don't forget to connect with other readers on social media with #lessonsthatlast

Story Theme Index

Lesson		Theme
44	Seeing Something Special	Affirmation
54	Knowing and Noting	Affirmation
64	Teaching Self-Advocacy	Affirmation
73	Nurturing Talent	Affirmation
75	Finding Strengths	Affirmation
120	Noticing a Knack	Affirmation
5	Being Authentic	Authenticity
37	Inspiring Self-Assurance	Authenticity
40	Making Musical Memories	Authenticity
86	Being Yourself	Authenticity
98	Being Human	Authenticity
165	Being Genuine	Authenticity
166	Getting Real	Authenticity
6	Being Memorable	Character
10	Developing Character	Character
17	Working Alongside	Character
27	Setting Boundaries	Character
77	Teaching More	Character
92	Inspiring Strength	Character
106	Being Present	Character
108	Teaching Resilience	Character
114	Fostering Growth	Character
115	Coaching Choice	Character
183	Starting Small	Character
1	Creating Tradition	Community
3	Being Brave	Community
11	Challenging Norms	Community
12	Teaching Civility	Community
20	Building Together	Community
25	Adding Some Fun	Community
31	Building Community	Community
63	Creating Space	Community
70	Inspiring Connections	Community
72	Providing Opportunity	Community
103	Coming Together	Community
123	Creating Bonds	Community
129	Building a Team	Community

(Continued)

Lesson		Theme
158	Broadening Perspectives	Community
172	Trusting Students	Community
185	Celebrating Goodbye	Community
13	Being There	Compassion
19	Giving Empathy	Compassion
32	Finding More	Compassion
67	Guiding and Providing	Compassion
85	Inspiring Perspective	Compassion
99	Assessing with Compassion	Compassion
111	Serving Together	Compassion
137	Reaching Out	Compassion
148	Warming Kindness	Compassion
150	Teaching Compassionately	Compassion
175	Serving While Learning	Compassion
2	Bringing the Light	Connection
33	Embracing Imperfections	Connection
51	Lasting Influence	Connection
78	Taking Time	Connection
93	Building Relationships	Connection
104	Showing Pride	Connection
112	Speaking Through Books	Connection
122	Accepting Appreciation	Connection
168	Staying Connected	Connection
180	Knowing Students	Connection
89	Embedding Instruction	Creativity
116	Exploring To Learn	Creativity
126	Deconstructing Principles	Creativity
128	Creating Joy	Creativity
139	Getting Creative	Creativity
144	Planning Positivity	Creativity
147	Bringing Joy	Creativity
149	Encouraging Freedom	Creativity
174	Launching Learning	Creativity
42	Moving to Learn	Delight
49	Making Memories	Delight
58	Making Magic	Delight
62	Going Big	Delight
91	Playing to Learn	Delight
124	Getting Playful	Delight
130	Supporting Social Skills	Delight
16	Making Friends	Empowerment
18	Friendly Encouragement	Empowerment
34	Making Flaws Fantastic	Empowerment
59	Instructing Implicitly	Empowerment
80	Cultivating Empowering Thoughts	Empowerment
117	Sharing Power	Empowerment

(Continued)

Lesson		Theme
132	Empowering Students	Empowerment
161	Inquiring Minds	Empowerment
162	Investigating Perceptions	Empowerment
8	Focusing on the Future	Encouragement
22	Leveraging Talents	Encouragement
23	Engaging in Positivity	Encouragement
24	Keeping the Faith	Encouragement
39	Rewarding Growth	Encouragement
41	Encouraging Growth	Encouragement
43	Checking In	Encouragement
47	Breaking Things Down	Encouragement
55	Getting Uncomfortable	Encouragement
79	Encouraging Confidence	Encouragement
83	Cheering Them On	Encouragement
94	Encouraging Goals	Encouragement
152	Encouraging Attempts	Encouragement
156	Partnering to Learn	Encouragement
163	Building Confidence	Encouragement
29	Real World Lessons	Engagement
35	Listening In	Engagement
60	Striking a Spark	Engagement
71	Giving Resources	Engagement
87	Igniting Passion	Engagement
90	Giving Options	Engagement
95	Creating Fun	Engagement
107	Seeing Wonders	Engagement
125	Preparing For Engagement	Engagement
151	Learning Preferences	Engagement
153	Providing Context	Engagement
170	Empowering Learners	Engagement
57	Being Tenacious	Expectations
61	Reinforcing Positivity	Expectations
110	Creating Community	Expectations
131	Building Foundations	Expectations
142	Reframing Assumptions	Expectations
176	Challenging More	Expectations
21	Embracing Individuality	Identity
30	Celebrating Individuality	Identity
56	Instilling Pride	Identity
65	Breaking Barriers	Identity
101	Becoming A Legacy	Identity
138	Understanding Representation	Identity
154	Crafting Opportunities	Identity
171	Connecting Community	Identity
173	Shifting Paradigms	Identity
14	Mining Potential	Inspiration

(Continued)

Lesson		Theme
26	Captivating Learners	Inspiration
28	Teaching that Echoes	Inspiration
48	Inspiring Outliers	Inspiration
66	Inspiring Pride	Inspiration
74	Impacting Futures	Inspiration
102	Inspiring Confidence	Inspiration
127	Encouraging Dreams	Inspiration
141	Building Family	Inspiration
164	Planting Seeds	Inspiration
4	Extending A Welcome	Kindness
7	Creating Nostalgia	Kindness
53	One Caring Adult	Kindness
68	Inspiring Adventure	Kindness
96	Sharing Time	Kindness
133	Speaking Encouragement	Kindness
50	Fostering Leadership	Leadership
134	Planning Success	Leadership
143	Investigating Complexity	Leadership
160	Learning by Telling	Leadership
36	Extending Kindness	Nurture
38	Sharing Wisdom	Nurture
81	Being Positive	Nurture
82	Becoming More	Nurture
113	Making A Difference	Nurture
45	Leveraging an Interest	Passion
52	Opening Doors	Passion
76	Discovering a Passion	Passion
105	Connecting Dots	Passion
118	Inspiring Passion	Passion
169	Clarifying Dreams	Passion
184	Lighting a Fire	Passion
9	Redirecting with Grace	Respect
15	Coaching Teamwork	Respect
84	Honoring Youth	Respect
136	Communicating Respect	Respect
155	Offering Choice	Respect
157	Providing Outlets	Respect
177	Valuing Voices	Respect
46	Providing Resources	Support
69	Opening Doors	Support
88	Noticing Change	Support
100	Sharing Strategies	Support
109	Showing Up	Support
119	Advocating For Students	Support
121	Waiving Judgment	Support
145	Encouraging Reflection	Support

(*Continued*)

Lesson		Theme
159	Starting Over	Support
178	Strategizing Together	Support
179	Noticing Needs	Support
181	Celebrating Gains	Support
182	Encouraging Action	Support
97	Understanding Needs	Worthiness
135	Paying Attention	Worthiness
140	Rewarding Effort	Worthiness
146	Building Esteem	Worthiness
167	Negating a Narrative	Worthiness

For Product Safety Concerns and Information please contact our EU
representative GPSR@taylorandfrancis.com
Taylor & Francis Verlag GmbH, Kaufingerstraße 24, 80331 München, Germany

www.ingramcontent.com/pod-product-compliance
Ingram Content Group UK Ltd.
Pitfield, Milton Keynes, MK11 3LW, UK
UKHW021450080625

459435UK00012B/441